# THE
# ROSARY

# THE
# ROSARY

## THE PRAYER THAT SAVED MY LIFE

# IMMACULÉE ILIBAGIZA

## with Steve Erwin

**HAY HOUSE, INC.**
Carlsbad, California • New York City
London • Sydney • Johannesburg
Vancouver • Hong Kong • New Delhi

*Published and distributed in the United States by:* Hay House, Inc.: www
.hayhouse.com® • *Published and distributed in Australia by:* Hay House
Australia Pty. Ltd.: www.hayhouse.com.au • *Published and distributed
in the United Kingdom by:* Hay House UK, Ltd.: www.hayhouse.co.uk •
*Published and distributed in the Republic of South Africa by:* Hay House SA
(Pty), Ltd.: www.hayhouse.co.za • *Distributed in Canada by:* Raincoast:
www.raincoast.com • *Published in India by:* Hay House Publishers India:
www.hayhouse.co.in

*Cover design:* Amy Rose Grigoriou • *Interior design:* Nick C. Welch

**Library of Congress Cataloging-in-Publication Data**

Ilibagiza, Immaculée.
  The Rosary : The Prayer That Saved My Life / Immaculée Ilibagiza,
with Steve Erwin. -- 1st edition.
    pages cm
  ISBN 978-1-4019-4017-1
  1. Rosary. 2. Catholic Church--Prayers and devotions.  I. Title.
  BX2163.I45 2013
  242'.74--dc23
                              2013014311


**Hardcover ISBN: 978-1-4019-4017-1**

16  15  14  13    4  3  2  1
1st edition, August 2013

Printed in the United States of America

*"The rosary is the most excellent form of prayer. . . .*
*It is the remedy for all our evils,*
*the root of all our blessings."*

— POPE LEO XIII

# CONTENTS

## PART III: THE LUMINOUS MYSTERIES

## PART IV: THE SORROWFUL MYSTERIES

## PART V: THE GLORIOUS MYSTERIES

# INTRODUCTION

## *Bending Heaven Toward Earth*

I sit down to write this book with a smile on my face and joy in my heart. With the exception of the precious moments I devote to praying the rosary each day, nothing gives me more happiness than discussing the beauty and power we can all bring into our lives when we pick up these sacred beads and turn our hearts toward heaven.

The power of the rosary will bring blessings into our lives too numerous to count. It can clear confusion from our thoughts, chase trouble from our hearts, resolve problems that plague us, restore us to health, and fill us with happiness and hope. Those are big promises to make and may sound too good to be true—I probably wouldn't believe them myself, except that they are promises that have been fulfilled in my own life and in the lives of countless other people.

The Virgin Mary, my favorite saint, promised that anyone who prays the rosary from their heart will receive anything their heart desires . . . and I am living proof that Our Lady keeps her promises.

I'VE HEARD COUNTLESS TESTIMONIALS about rosary prayers transforming lives shattered by despair, healing bodies ravaged by sickness, curing addiction, and reviving hearts withered by hatred, loneliness, and betrayal. I have seen the rosary work wonders in the lives of people all over the world, be they Catholic or non-Catholic, or even those who have little to no religious belief at all. So please know that this is not a book solely for Catholics; it is a book for anyone who has faith in God and who believes prayers can be answered.

I assure you, prayers are always answered when offered by a humble, believing heart—no matter how trivial or how great the request may be. The rosary can and will bring you everything you need to live a happy and prosperous life, as long as you pray with faith and sincerity. And, amazingly, it only takes 20 minutes a day!

But make no mistake, the rosary is not magic; it is faith in action. Jesus told us that with faith only the size of a mustard seed, any one of us can move mountains. The rosary is a tool that focuses our prayers and helps us develop our faith to the point that we can get those mountains moving. It is a tool that will deepen and strengthen our relationship with God, and in doing so all the treasure heaven has to offer can be ours.

These are no idle boasts; the enormity of the rosary's power has been well documented throughout history. As we will look at later, the Virgin Mary, according to legend, presented the first rosary to St. Dominic de Guzman in the 13th century to combat the sin and heresy of his age. Since then the Blessed Mother has appeared to saints and visionaries across the centuries telling us of the rosary's immense powers. She appeared to the children of Fátima in Portugal, promising that World War I would end and millions of lives would be spared if people prayed the rosary. She appeared to the young visionaries in Rwanda in the early 1980s, promising the genocide could be avoided if everyone prayed the rosary to cleanse hatred from their hearts. We didn't listen, and 12 years after she gave her warning the country was destroyed by genocide as she had predicted.

As you can see, the rosary has enormous power: power that can change the world; that can defeat evil; and that, perhaps most important of all, can bring a permanent peace to our hearts. I should know. I would not be here today if not for the prayers of the rosary—which literally saved my life.

For those of you who don't know me, my name is Immaculée and I am a survivor of the bloody 1994 genocide that devastated my beautiful African homeland of Rwanda. I was a 24-year-old university student when a government-backed holocaust of unimaginable evil was unleashed upon my country's minority tribe, the Tutsis. To be Tutsi in Rwanda, like my family was, was a death sentence. In less than 100 days almost the entire Tutsi population of Rwanda—more than one million innocent men, women, and children—were mercilessly tortured, raped, and butchered during what is now acknowledged as one of the most vicious campaigns of ethnic cleansing in human history. Almost every member of my immediate and extended family was murdered during the slaughter, and so was just about every other person I had ever loved or called a friend.

I survived, thanks to the kindness of a local pastor who took mercy upon me and seven other Tutsi women by hiding us in a tiny bathroom for three months. The pastor's kindness prevented me from being murdered, but it was the prayers of the rosary that saved my life, and my soul.

My experiences during the genocide and its aftermath are chronicled in my first two books, *Left to Tell: Discovering God Amidst the Rwandan Holocaust* and *Led By*

*Faith: Rising from the Ashes of the Rwandan Genocide.* If you are interested in how faith and forgiveness became my guiding lights in a world darkened by hatred and despair, please read them both.

In this book, I want to share with you how praying the rosary saved my life during three months when fear and despair were my constant companions and worst enemies as killers hunted me, thoughts of suicide plagued me, and the devil whispered in my ear.

With the rosary I was, even during the darkest days of my life, able to find God and fill my heart with a love that enabled me to forgive those who killed my family and move on to lead a full and happy life. Of course, like everyone else, my life is far from perfect: I experience setbacks and heartaches, and battle my own doubts and insecurities. But I know from experience that praying the rosary will bring me closer to God, and the closer I am to Him, the more His love will sustain and uplift me, no matter how hopeless things may seem.

God has promised us great things if we pray the rosary faithfully, and if I am certain of anything, it is that God never lies or fails to keep His word.

I AM SO DEVOTED TO THE ROSARY and assured of its protective power that I never leave home without my beads and even sleep with them in my hand. I am not a rosary fanatic, but as you will see in the coming pages, I am a true believer in its power to transform hearts and souls! Today as I travel the world sharing my story at seminars, conferences, and retreats, I am continually asked how I survived the genocide. My short answer is always the same: "It was the rosary. The rosary is the prayer that saved my life."

But the rosary's done so much more for me than that— it has given me a life filled with peace and hope, and the knowledge that if I pray it properly and with all my heart, I can overcome any obstacle and fulfill every dream. And, as you will soon discover, you can, too.

The rosary has been described as a rope that bends heaven toward Earth. It is my deepest desire that when you reach the end of this book and are joyously praying the rosary with all of your heart, you will feel that heaven really is a little bit closer.

# PART I

# GROWING UP WITH THE ROSARY

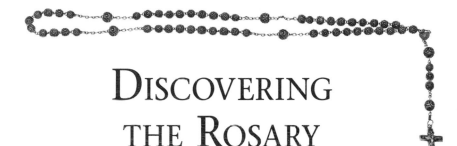

# CHAPTER 1

# DISCOVERING THE ROSARY

Even though I've been asked the question hundreds of times, I'm still a little amazed when someone wants me to describe what the rosary is. I have three different reactions when the question is put to me. At first I'm both a bit shocked and a tad saddened, realizing that not everyone was as lucky as I was to have been exposed to the rosary in childhood. But when the surprise passes, I am delighted to produce a rosary from my pocket and talk about my favorite subject. And then, for a moment at least, I am inexplicably tongue-tied by the enormity of the question—it's like being asked to explain what the ocean is. I could say that the ocean is a huge body of salt water, which is a simple and accurate answer. Or I could give a more meaningful reply, explaining that the ocean is God's gift to us, the source of life that brings the rain to our crops and helps to warm and cool our planet. Without the ocean, life on Earth would be impossible.

I could answer the question about the rosary in much the same way. I could hold it out in the palm of my hand and say, "As you can see, it is a string of prayer beads." Or, I could say, "It is a string of prayer beads that, like the ocean, is a gift to us from God. It was presented to us by the Virgin Mary. When we pray with it the way the Blessed Mother instructed us, it will sustain us and our spirit will flourish. And without prayer, a spiritual life is impossible."

Of course, that still wouldn't answer the question properly or enough. So what I do, and have done on so many occasions, is to sit down and share the story about how I came to know and learn about the rosary. And if you will allow me, that is what I'd love to do with you right now.

I PROBABLY FIRST HEARD THE GENTLE RATTLE of my parents' prayer beads on the very day I was born. Both of my parents loved to pray the rosary, but my father was especially devoted to the daily practice of using the beads to connect with God, Jesus, and the Virgin Mary.

My dad was raised as a Protestant, but as a young man converted to Catholicism because (among other reasons) when he read the Bible he fell in love with the purity radiating from the heart of the Virgin Mary. In Rwanda's Catholic Church he found a place where Mary was truly venerated and the rosary was accepted and encouraged in an individual's public and private prayer life.

When I was still an infant Mom, Dad, and my two older brothers—Damascene and Aimable—prayed the rosary together, kneeling as a family on the living room floor. By the time I was four years old I had a rosary of my own and was praying with the rest of my family. I just accepted that this was a part of my life. I cannot recall a single instance from my childhood when I felt awkward or embarrassed when, no matter where we were, my family would pull out our rosaries and begin praying together. If we went to visit relatives in a neighboring village, you could be certain that the hours-long car ride would be passed reciting rosary prayers.

When I was old enough to walk to school on my own, I carried a rosary in my hand and prayers on my lips the entire eight-mile hike there and back. To ensure we were never without a rosary, or had spares if an unexpected guest dropped by during prayers, my parents kept extra rosaries tucked away in cubbyholes all over the house. This may make my folks sound like religious zealots, but nothing could be further from the truth. They were very balanced in their religious beliefs—devoutly Catholic, but universal in their Christian beliefs and always did unto others as they would have others do unto them. What made them special, in my eyes and in my heart, was their love for the Virgin Mary and for Mary's special affinity for the rosary. I believe that my father knew that the rosary was one of the greatest tools of prayer and devotion available to humankind. He did everything in his power to instill within his family, friends, and community the same love and fervor he had for the rosary.

I'm also aware that the first impression many have of the rosary is of people sitting in dark churches mumbling Hail Marys in an endless, repetitive monotone. But I never thought of the rosary as a dull recitation of meaningless words, not even as a rambunctious child who loved playing outside more than anything. No, to me the sound of that lovely prayer to the Blessed Mother—*Hail Mary, full of grace, the Lord is with thee; blessed art thou among women, and blessed is the fruit of thy womb, Jesus. Holy Mary, Mother of God, pray for us sinners, now and at the hour of our death*—landed softly upon my ears like sweet music floating down from heaven. Besides, praying made me feel good . . . I felt special, I felt loved, and I felt protected. Any form of prayer filled me with a warmth and sense of well-being that was always strongest when praying the rosary with my family. It was as though every cell in my body was absorbing peace and happiness as I listened to the prayers being recited, and I often found my eyes welling with tears.

In all honesty, I really didn't know what all the prayers meant when I was child, and I couldn't commit more than one or two of them to memory. More often than not I just repeated the Hail Mary and listened to my parents and older brothers recite the other prayers. I guess the problem for me was that most of the rosary prayers are contemplative; you have to think about certain Bible stories and events between reciting the Hail Marys. Well, deep meditation wasn't my strong suit as a child; instead, I preferred getting lost in the beautiful words and rhythm of the Hail Mary prayer. I didn't feel the need to probe the depths of the words or dwell upon the stories. At that point in my life it didn't matter to me what I was saying as long as I was part of my family's prayers and a member in good standing in the family of God. I had a blessed childhood—I was a very, very happy little girl. I loved my family, I loved God, I loved praying, and more and more, I was growing in my love for the Virgin Mary.

ONE DAY WHEN I WAS TEN, I actually did start to think about the prayers I was saying, and instead of feeling warm all over, I was filled with doubt. I have no idea why my faith in God was shaken, but it was . . . and shaken to its very core. Suddenly Bible stories and the words of our local priest rang hollow and false. How could anyone *know* that God existed for a fact? How could we verify events that happened in a strange place called Israel 2,000 years before any living person had been born? How could water be turned into wine; or 5 fishes feed 5,000; or anyone rise from the dead? Who was it we were all getting on our knees to pray to anyway—an invisible old man who was everyone's father who floated in the clouds, writing down every good or bad thing we did every single day? How was that even remotely possible?

Anyone who had seen or heard Jesus speak had been dead and buried for centuries, and as far as I could tell there was no way to prove anything that was written in the Bible or anything the Church claimed to be true. The depths of my disbelief grew daily and, because I had been so devout and happy in my belief in God, I became inwardly miserable. I knew my parents took great joy in my love of prayer, and I dared not reveal to them my doubts and inner turmoil.

I spent weeks trying to convince myself God was real. Rwanda is often called "the land of a thousand hills" because the landscape of the country consists of an endless series of valleys and rolling hills and low mountains. During this troubled time I would drag my schoolmates up to a different mountaintop each day after class to get closer to heaven and put some tough questions to God. (I may have been skeptical, but I was still just a kid with a kid's imagination!) When we reached the top of the mountain, I'd pray for answers—but none came to me and I truly began to despair.

Perhaps my cynicism was simply the logical, rational side of my adult brain developing and asserting itself in my consciousness, forcing me to question everything I had been told and taught. Maybe it was a surge of hormones released during an early puberty, or just something I ate, I don't know. I have written about my bout of youthful skepticism in my book *Our Lady of Kibeho,* and won't go into it in greater detail here, except to say that if my doubts about the existence of God had continued for any significant length of time, I would have likely descended into a depression from which I never would have emerged.

Thank God He heard my prayers and found a way to ease my troubled mind with a story that involved the rosary. I recounted this story in detail in *Our Lady of Kibeho* and will say here only that, after enduring long months of spiritual angst, Miss Odette, a Protestant teacher at my Catholic grade school, inadvertently restored my faith by teaching the class the story of Our Lady of Fátima.

If you are not familiar with this wonderful story, it is about a series of visitations the Virgin Mary made to three young shepherd children near the remote Portuguese village of Fátima in 1917. I had never heard of supernatural visitations before and pressed Miss Odette for details. She told the class about the Blessed Mother's visit to Fátima and her urging the children to pray the rosary, and to encourage others to pray with all their hearts as well.

Miss Odette told my classmates and me that, while no one other than the three children saw Mary, tens of thousands of people traveled to the visitation site to witness the young shepherds experiencing their miraculous apparitions. Many who came saw other wonders, like the sun zooming toward the earth and, after a sudden downpour, drying soaked clothing and muddy puddles in a matter of minutes—events investigators were at a loss to explain. All of this had happened in the lifetime of people still living; and had been reported in newspapers, investigated and verified by doctors and scientists, and ultimately approved by the Church itself after its own investigation! Miss Odette then told us about other apparitions of Mary through the ages, including those to Bernadette of Lourdes, where once again, the rosary played a central theme in Our Lady's supernatural visit.

After hearing all of this, my doubts were put to rest. If so many people had witnessed these supernatural things, and if doctors and scientists who were not easily fooled said it was really true, and if the Church's own experts approved of the visions . . . well, then that was good enough for me. If Mary came to see us from heaven, then heaven existed! My faith in God was forever restored, and I once again believed what my parents, teachers, priests, and the Bible told me about God.

And then I decided to become a visionary myself. I recruited two young friends to form a group of three children, just like the Fátima shepherds. We climbed to the top of a hill every day in the fall of 1981 and prayed the rosary for Mary to appear to us. Believe it or not (as you will already know if you've read *Our Lady of Kibeho*), while we were standing on that hill, the Virgin Mary did come to Rwanda! She didn't appear to us, though, but to several young schoolgirls in the village of Kibeho, just a few hours' drive from my parents' house. She urged all Rwandans to pray the rosary every day to avoid a great "river of blood" that would flow over our country if we did not stop hating one another. Sadly, we didn't heed her warning, and that river of blood was indeed unleashed during the genocide.

The Kibeho visitations have been thoroughly investigated, documented, and approved by the Vatican. And while I was disappointed that the Blessed Mother didn't visit me personally, the fact that she came to Rwanda at all has forever etched my love for her upon my heart.

ONCE MARY BEGAN VISITING KIBEHO and urging all of God's children to pray the rosary daily, I resolved to learn the rosary prayers I had only semi-learned and had been half saying for so many years. By coincidence (or, I prefer to think, by divine intervention) the Blessed Mother's arrival in Rwanda occurred around the time I was to receive the Sacrament of Confirmation. Before I would be allowed to participate in that sacred rite, an event that would mark my adult entry into the Church as a fully practicing Catholic, I needed a complete knowledge of the Church's sacraments, rites, and prayers—including the rosary. To prove that I was ready for this solemn event I, along with scores of other 12- and 13-year-olds, had to report to the parish priest and successfully pass a confirmation exam, the most difficult section of which was the dreaded "rosary test."

It was a test I vowed to pass with flying colors.

# CHAPTER 2

# GETTING A
# HISTORY LESSON

The moment I started studying for my rosary test, the daily angst and frequent nightmares that accompanied my youthful loss of faith vanished. It was then that I began my lifelong practice of falling asleep with a rosary in my hand and waking each morning refreshed, with a smile on my face and a prayer in my heart.

Not only did the dark days of doubt disappear from my life, but I was also happier than ever—and what's more, everyone around me seemed happier as well. People in our village were getting along better than usual, even the grumpiest of villagers stopped on the road to extend greetings and hugs with neighbors they hadn't spoken to for years. At first I thought the change was due to my new devotion to the rosary. But soon I discovered the community's shifting mood was due to something much larger than my personal prayer routine . . . and the credit belonged entirely to Our Lady.

You see, the Blessed Mother's first appearance at the all-girls' high school in Kibeho was soon followed by many more visitations. When Mary appeared, the schoolgirl visionaries—Alphonsine, Anathalie, and Marie-Claire

—would enter a trancelike ecstasy that could last for hours, during which they were completely impervious to their surroundings. Scientists and doctors tried to prove that the students were faking by sticking needles into their bodies, shining blinding lights directly into their eyes, and many other foolproof physical tests, all of which verified that the seers were indeed in an "otherworldly" state.

The most wonderful thing about the girls' visions of Mary was that they shared them with all of us. Alphonsine, Anathalie, and Marie-Claire repeated the messages Mary had brought from heaven, and many of those messages were about the incredible blessings bestowed upon those praying the rosary with sincerity. The crowds making the pilgrimage to Kibeho to listen to Mary's messages swelled from a few hundred to several thousand, and just about every one of them was praying a rosary during their journey. Praying the rosary had become the latest fashion!

ONE MORNING I RAN INTO FATHER RWAGEMA, our village priest, who had made the pilgrimage to see the visionaries of Kibeho several times. He was carrying an armful of rosaries of every length and color. He told me that people from our village and the surrounding villages had given them to him to take to Kibeho to be blessed by the Virgin Mary.

By that time, the crowds were so big—about 30,000 at every apparition—that the local authorities built a podium for Alphonsine, Anathalie, and Marie-Claire to stand on during the apparitions. Father Rwagema placed his pile of rosaries at the edge of the podium and at some point during the apparitions the Holy Mother blessed them all.

"I've been doing this for weeks now," Father Rwagema told me. "Haven't you noticed how happy everybody seems? It is because they are all praying the rosary!"

I ran home and gathered together all of my family's rosary beads and ran back to Father Rwagema to have them blessed by Mary. There was nothing I wanted more than to accompany him to Kibeho and listen to the visionaries myself. What better place to learn the proper way to pray Mary's favorite prayer than sitting at her feet while she appeared to schoolgirls who were just like me?

Yet that dream was not to be. My parents refused my repeated requests to take me to Kibeho or to let me go with Father Rwagema. There was no proper road leading to the remote village, and pilgrimages (which made the three-day journey on foot) had to pass through wild and dangerous country. If I did manage to arrive safely, my parents worried that I would get lost among—or even crushed to death by—the enormous crowd of fervent pilgrims. They were worried (and now that I'm a parent myself I couldn't agree more with them!) about the safety of their precious only daughter. They made it clear that I could never change their minds on the topic, so I contented myself by listening to Radio Rwanda broadcast the highlights of the visionaries relaying Mary's messages, or by listening to the tapes Father Rwagema made of the visionaries during his pilgrimages.

Thankfully our priest was always true to his word. One evening after returning from Kibeho, he knocked on our door carrying the family rosaries I had entrusted to him.

"Did she?!" I asked him in the doorway before even inviting him into our home—a major faux pas when it comes to rules of Rwandan hospitality. "Did Mary bless our beads?"

"Of course she did, child," the kindly priest said with a smile, handing me my own small wooden-beaded rosary. He then reached into his jacket and produced another special gift for me—a small, illustrated booklet containing all the prayers and "mysteries" of the rosary. "To help you study for your big test," Father Rwagema said, still smiling.

I thanked him profusely and then immediately retreated to my room, flopped onto my bed, and opened the pages of my new rosary book with one hand while marveling at the beautiful beads I gently held in the other. I would treasure that rosary as a prized possession until the day I was forced to flee our home when the genocide erupted. That rosary, along with everything else I owned, was either stolen or destroyed in the bloody mayhem of that terrible time.

On that splendid evening, though, life could not have been any better—I was a happy 12-year-old sitting in the safety of a loving home with doting parents and brothers looking out for me as I read stories about the life of Jesus and his family, with a rosary that had just been blessed by the Queen of Heaven herself pressed against my grateful heart.

My study guide was a wonderful tool that taught me a bit of the history of the rosary and the basics of how to use the beads to pray. That little book, filled with diagrams and pictures of the Holy Family, helped me understand the meaning of what I had been saying by rote during family prayers since I was a toddler.

Using Father Rwagema's study guide, as well as talking to both him and Father Clement, another local priest who was a dear friend to our family, I began to get a good sense of the origins and importance of the rosary.

WHAT I CAME TO UNDERSTAND from the priests and my book (and I caution the reader that this is a personal interpretation—I am not a biblical scholar or an academic or an expert on the rosary), a form of the rosary has been used in prayers for hundreds and hundreds of years.

Father Clement, who had studied at a seminary and was a very learned man, told me that monks and other religious devotees used to tie knots in the rope they used as belts to tighten their robes as a type of rosary, to count the psalms they recited each day—and because they usually prayed the entire 150 psalms of the Bible, they needed a way to keep track. Since everyone thirsted for God and ways to communicate with the Lord, the monks' prayers were soon adopted by ordinary people. However, because most men and women back then couldn't read or write, learning 150 psalms was an impossible task, so it was replaced with 150 repetitions of the Lord's Prayer, a devotion known as "the Paternoster." And because the common folk loved the Virgin Mary so much, they replaced the Our Father prayers by repeating the Hail Mary 150 times, which was known as "the Psalter of Our Lady."

"You don't really need to know any of the history, my child," Father Clement said to me when I kept pestering him to explain more about the rosary. He told me to just pray as often as I could, and to thoroughly read the rosary book Father Rwagema gave me to prepare for my test. "Right now, you will find everything you need to know about the rosary in the pages of that book," he assured me.

My rosary book started by recounting the story of St. Dominic, the founder of the Order of Preachers (also known as the Dominican Order), who was born in Spain in 1170. The book had a picture of the gentle-looking Dominic, whose compassion for those suffering around him was so great that he sold all his worldly possessions, including his clothing, to shelter the poor and feed the hungry. Dominic worked tirelessly to serve the Virgin Mary and spread the word of Christ at home and in distant lands where people still worshipped pagan idols.

According to tradition, the Virgin Mary came to Dominic in a vision and presented him with a rosary much like we have today, urging him to use it to combat heresy and convert the hearts of sinners. My little book described how the rosary has been used by countless saints and holy people in prayer, veneration, and to work miracles. One of the pictures in the book was of the Virgin Mary appearing to Bernadette of Lourdes, with a long rosary draped around her arm. There was a beautiful quote beneath a picture of Our Lady of Fátima attributed to Sister Lucia, one of the young shepherd children the Blessed Mother appeared to in Fátima. It read: "My impression is that Our Lady wanted to give ordinary people who might not know how to pray this simple method of getting closer to God. There is no problem, I tell you, no matter how difficult it is, that we cannot solve by the prayer of the Holy Rosary."

There were many other quotes about the rosary from popes and saints throughout history, some of which I remember clearly all these years later. There was one from Pope Adrian VI, who lived about 500 years ago and said, "The rosary is the scourge of the devil." In the mid-1800s, Pope Pius IX, who later become a saint, believed in the power of the rosary so much that he proclaimed, "Give me an army saying the rosary and I will conquer the world." The very next pope, Leo XIII, said the rosary was "the most excellent form of prayer . . . . It is the remedy for all our evils, the root of all our blessings." At the beginning of the 20th century, Pope Pius X, another pope to be made a saint, called the rosary "the most beautiful and richest of all prayers to [Mary]; it is the prayer that touches most the heart of the Mother of God. Say it each day!"

And my favorite pope of all time, John Paul II, who was declared pope just a few years before the Blessed Mother began appearing in Rwanda, announced that the rosary was his favorite prayer and urged everyone to pray it fervently each day.

Perhaps the most memorable quote I read was from the 17th- and 18th-century French priest St. Louis-Marie de Montfort, who wrote the famous book *The Secret of the Rosary*. He said that even if you've committed just about every sin in the book and "even if you are on the brink of damnation, even if you have one foot in hell," praying the rosary with faith every day until you die will get you into heaven.

*Wow!* I thought. *That is one powerful set of prayer beads!*

The opening pages and those amazing quotes from some of the most famous men in the history of religion made an enormous impression on my young mind, which was thirsting to drink in everything there was to know about these incredible beads the Blessed Mother carried all the way from heaven eight centuries ago to give to St. Dominic. Maybe it was the ability the rosary had to fascinate such powerful men throughout time that made me develop such a keen interest in what some considered to be just a string of beads. Or perhaps it was the supernatural qualities attributed to the rosary that fired my imagination and made me such a passionate enthusiast. When I look back at that period of my life now, I tend to think all the little "unrelated" rosary events happening all around me were part of the Blessed Mother's plan to prepare me for the dark days to come in just 12 short years, when it would be the rosary I would reach for to save my life.

Whatever the reasons, I set about studying the rosary with a new reverence and renewed determination. Looking down at my study book and seeing everything I had to learn made me realize that to master the rosary and ensure I passed my upcoming rosary test, I must do something that up until then had completely eluded me—I had to memorize all of the rosary prayers and mysteries, and I had to memorize them in their proper order.

*Oh my God,* I thought. *That is going to take a miracle!*

# CHAPTER 3

# LEARNING
# THE BASICS

When I went to university, my classes mainly consisted of advanced mathematics and science, which required excellent memorization skills. The irony of this made me laugh at the time because when I was 12 years old, memorizing just the 7 short prayers and 15 mysteries of the rosary utterly confounded me. Maybe the creative side of my brain was overly active back then, but I seemed to lack the logic needed to remember things in an ordered fashion.

Thank goodness I was stubborn, though—once I'd set my mind to do something, one way or another I would get it done. So, every day after school I set aside about an hour to memorize all I needed to know to pass my upcoming rosary test. I opened my study guide, carefully spread my rosary beads alongside the book, and then proceeded to look from book to beads and back again, hoping something would stick in my brain. The first thing I learned about the rosary was that it was going to take me a while to learn it.

FOR THOSE OF YOU WHO DON'T KNOW too much about the subject at hand, let me provide a very brief description. The traditional Catholic rosary I am discussing in this book is, in the most basic sense, a stringed circlet (the string is usually a piece of cord or a delicate metal chain) of evenly spaced plastic, wood, or glass beads of various sizes. An additional small bit of beaded string or chain extends from the bottom of the circlet, to which a crucifix is attached. (Please see the illustration later in the chapter.)

The beads are divided into sets used to keep track of the prayers associated with the rosary. The number of prayers can vary slightly depending on local custom, but I learned using seven prayers—although some of the prayers are repeated many times.

Besides the Rosary Prayers, there are also Rosary Mysteries, which are condensed versions of the most important stories and events in the lives of Jesus and Mary, which should be reflected upon between saying certain sets of prayers. But at this point in my studying, I decided to focus on the prayers—so we will get to the mysteries a little bit later.

The first assignment I gave myself was memorizing the seven prayers and remembering whether they were prayed while holding the crucifix or holding the beads . . . and if it was the beads, *which* beads.

To help my memorization, I drew a rosary on a piece of paper and marked down which part of it—the crucifix or the beads—each prayer belonged to. I discovered that the prayer we say the most often is the Hail Mary, which we pray a total of 53 times on 53 individual beads! The Hail Mary beads are divided into six sets—five separate sets of ten beads each, called decades, and one additional set of three beads.

Between each of the five decades of Hail Mary beads, and on either side of the three-bead set of Hail Mary beads, we find one slightly larger bead—so in total there are six larger beads. On the larger beads we pray the Glory Be Prayer, the Fátima Prayer, and the Our Father Prayer (or as many, including me, call it—the Lord's Prayer).

On the crucifix, where we begin praying the rosary, we say two prayers. The first is the Sign of the Cross, which is a gesture *and* a prayer, and the second is the Apostles' Creed.

And, at the very end of the rosary, we say the Hail Holy Queen Prayer.

While all those prayers sounded a little complicated to me at first, it was the easiest part of the rosary for me to memorize. There were only seven prayers, some of which I already knew by heart. But to be thorough, I wrote each prayer out to make sure I had everything committed to memory.

My prayer list looked like this:

Prayers to Learn for the Big Test:

## THE SIGN OF THE CROSS

*In the name of the Father, and the Son,*
*and the Holy Spirit. Amen.*

## THE APOSTLES' CREED

*I believe in God, the Father Almighty,*
*Creator of heaven and earth;*
*and in Jesus Christ, His only son, Our Lord;*
*who was conceived by the Holy Spirit, born of the*
*Virgin Mary, suffered under Pontius Pilate,*
*was crucified, died, and was buried.*
*He descended into hell; the third day he*
*rose again from the dead;*
*he ascended into heaven, and sits at the right hand of God,*
*the Father almighty; from thence he shall come to judge*
*the living and the dead.*
*I believe in the Holy Spirit, the holy Catholic Church,*
*the communion of saints, the forgiveness of sins,*
*the resurrection of the body and life everlasting. Amen.*

## THE LORD'S PRAYER
## (THE OUR FATHER PRAYER)

*Our Father, Who art in heaven,*
*Hallowed be Thy name.*
*Thy Kingdom come,*
*Thy will be done*
*on earth as it is in heaven.*
*Give us this day our daily bread,*
*and forgive us our trespasses,*
*as we forgive those who trespass against us.*
*And lead us not into temptation,*
*but deliver us from evil.*
*Amen.*

## THE HAIL MARY PRAYER

*Hail Mary, full of grace,*
*the Lord is with thee.*
*Blessed art thou among women,*
*and blessed is the fruit*
*of thy womb, Jesus.*
*Holy Mary, Mother of God,*
*pray for us sinners,*
*now and at the hour of our death.*
*Amen.*

## THE GLORY BE PRAYER

*Glory be to the Father,*
*and to the Son,*
*and to the Holy Spirit.*
*As it was in the beginning*
*is now and ever shall be,*
*world without end.*
*Amen.*

## THE FÁTIMA PRAYER

*O my Jesus, forgive us our sins, save us from the fires of hell,*
*and lead all souls to heaven, especially those*
*who are most in need of your mercy.*

## HAIL HOLY QUEEN PRAYER

*Hail Holy Queen, Mother of Mercy, our life,*
*our sweetness, and our hope.*
*To thee do we cry, poor banished children of Eve.*
*To thee do we send up our sighs, mourning and weeping*
*in this valley of tears.*
*Turn, then, most gracious advocate, thine eyes of mercy*
*toward us, and after this, our exile, show unto us*
*the blessed fruit of thy womb, Jesus.*
*O clement, O loving, O sweet Virgin Mary.*

That was it for the prayers. Although some were said more often than others, there were only seven prayers I had to know by heart. Drilling them into my head through constant practice is, I'm sure, what prepped my brain for memorizing the formulas and equations I needed as I advanced in school.

Yet both Father Clement and Father Rwagema cautioned me to not get caught up in just memorizing prayers to pass my test because I might lose sight of the prayers' real meaning.

One day Father Clement even read a Bible passage to me when he found me in my front yard rapidly murmuring my rosary prayers with my eyes squeezed shut and hands over my ears to block out distractions.

"Immaculée, if I may interrupt," he said. "I am so proud of you for taking your prayers seriously, but, child, a little advice—make sure you understand what you're saying. A good prayer is what pleases God, and good prayers come from the heart, not the head. Listen to this passage from the Gospel of Matthew, as it is Jesus instructing us how *not* to pray: *And when you pray, do not keep on babbling like pagans, for they think they will be heard because of their many words."*

Father Clement explained to me that pagans were people who didn't believe in Jesus and often worshipped idols. He said pagans believed that the quantity of their words outweighed the quality of their prayers because a longer prayer meant a greater reward from a happy idol.

"I want you to remember Jesus's words when you begin to study the mysteries because the mysteries are not to be memorized and rattled off like a shopping list. They are the key events of Christ's life. You must contemplate them, meditate upon them, and reflect on the meaning they have both for daily life and for your life everlasting."

The priest smiled and patted me on the head and left me in the yard to finish my studies. As he entered our house to visit with my parents, he turned and said, "Remember Our Savior's words . . . and don't be in such a hurry to learn everything. The rosary is a sweet and happy prayer—that's why it is named after a bouquet of roses. Take the time to enjoy it!"

As profound as Father Clement was, and as seriously as I took his advice, he had just reminded me that I still had to memorize an entire other part of the rosary—the mysteries! And at that moment I realized I didn't even really know what they were.

FROM PRAYING WITH MY FAMILY, reading my rosary book, and talking with Fathers Clement and Rwagema, I gathered that the Rosary Mysteries were primarily stories from the New Testament describing key events in the life of Jesus, events that often happened when the Blessed Mother was with her son.

The mysteries were divided into three sets—Joyful, Sorrowful, and Glorious. Today, thanks to an additional set that was added to the rosary in 2002 by Pope John Paul II (the Luminous Mysteries), there are now four sets of mysteries attached to the rosary. Each set describes five events, which add up to a total of 20 mystery stories. But when I was studying the beads as a girl, there were only three sets of mysteries, which meant 15 stories for me to memorize—and that was more than enough for me to tackle at the time!

First of all, I was told that they were called "mysteries" because some of the events they described were miraculous and beyond human understanding, such as the Virgin Birth. Unlike the Lord's Prayer or the Apostles' Creed, the three sets of mysteries were not in fact prayers per se.

In other words, we don't actually say a prayer named after the main events in Jesus's life, but we are encouraged to reflect upon these events for as long as we like—be it a minute or a day, depending on what is happening in our life at the time—just before we say the ten Hail Mary Prayers on each decade of the rosary. There are five decades on the rosary, and each decade corresponds to a key event in Our Lord's life and the life of the Blessed Mother.

So, when I put the prayers and the mysteries together I had my first view of how we are supposed to pray the rosary, which is as follows:

- First we say the first two prayers on the crucifix, the Sign of the Cross (while crossing ourselves) and the Apostles' Creed.

- We then move to the first large bead above the crucifix and say the Lord's Prayer.

- On each of next three smaller beads we say the Hail Mary.

- On the next large bead we say the Glory Be and the Fátima Prayer and announce which mystery we intend to reflect upon; for example, the Annunciation. We take as much time as we need to meditate on the mystery and reflect upon what it means, and then say the Lord's Prayer.

- Next we move on to the first decade and recite ten Hail Marys (one for each bead of the decade), until we reach the end of that decade.

- Then we start all over again, this time saying the Glory Be and the Fátima Prayer on the next large bead—where we announce the next mystery, meditate and reflect upon it, and then say the Lord's Prayer.

- Then we move to the next decade, where we say ten Hail Marys (one on each bead).

- The process continues until we complete the entire rosary, which we finish by saying the Glory Be, the Fátima Prayer, and the Hail Holy Queen Prayer; then we make and say the Sign of the Cross.

My poor brain rebelled at the prospect of remembering all that, but I took comfort in knowing I had already learned all of the prayers. Now, I just had to commit the 15 mysteries to memory and remember the order they went in. This would prove to be my greatest challenge because, while I'd heard my parents say the mysteries during family prayers, they all sounded the same to me and I usually just tuned out. I found the mysteries confusing in their content and their numbering; and to make matters worse, certain mysteries were only to be prayed on certain days of the week!

After reading and rereading the mystery stories, I could sort of remember what the stories were about—Jesus as a boy getting lost, Jesus on the Cross, the Virgin Mary visiting her cousin, the apostles witnessing Jesus ascending to heaven—but I couldn't for the life of me get a clear idea in my head of what order the stories came in or to which set of mysteries each story belonged.

I sat in the backyard ready to give up, when I said out loud in exasperation, "Mary, you should be here to help me remember how these stories go . . . after all, you were there in the first place!"

A few minutes later, a family passed by along the road in front of me. There was the dad in the lead followed by six kids, three boys and three girls, all walking in single file. They were also apparently walking in the order of their birth: the one in the front behind the dad was tallest, and they progressively dropped in height, with the shortest child bringing up the rear. And at the very back was the mom carrying a baby on her back. I was struck by how oddly regimented they looked. Then it hit me—I had the answer to my problem! I could remember the order of the mysteries by putting them in groups and in chronological order! Boys with boys, girls with girls, and in order from eldest to youngest, or vice versa.

It may sound silly, but it was a huge breakthrough for me. Realizing that the mysteries could be memorized in this way made mastering the rosary seem possible to me once again. Sure, there were still 15 stories and three sets of events to remember, but events that occurred chronologically! And stories similar to each other could be grouped together—Joyful Mysteries had to be joyful, right? The Sorrowful Mysteries must all be sad, and the Glorious Mysteries, well, they would be glorious in some way.

I immediately wrote down the title of each group, as well as descriptions of the events in the life of Jesus and Mary they described. Voilá! I had mastered the Mysteries of the Rosary. I smiled with relief and in amazement as I surveyed my list; it seemed so childishly simple to me now, and I just couldn't understand why I had been so baffled. *Oh well,* I thought, *I guess that's part of the mystery!*

My new list looked like this:

## THE JOYFUL MYSTERIES

### 1. The Annunciation

The Angel Gabriel announces to Mary that she has been chosen to be the mother of Jesus.

### 2. The Visitation

Mary, now pregnant with Jesus, goes to visit her cousin Elizabeth, who is pregnant with John the Baptist.

### 3. The Nativity

Jesus is born in Bethlehem.

### 4. The Presentation

Mary and Joseph take the infant Jesus to the
temple in Jerusalem to present him to God.

### 5. The Finding of Jesus in the Temple

The 12-year-old Jesus is lost in Jerusalem.
After searching for him for three days,
Mary and Joseph find him in the temple,
discussing theology with priests.

## THE SORROWFUL MYSTERIES

### 1. The Agony in the Garden

Jesus prays in the Garden of Gethsemane
on the night before he is put to death. He
struggles to accept his fate, and sweats beads
of blood.

### 2. The Scourging at the Pillar

Jesus is tied to a pillar and scourged on
Pilate's orders.

### 3. The Crowning of Thorns

Jesus is crowned with thorns after being
beaten and scourged.

### 4. The Carrying of the Cross

After being scourged and crowned with
thorns, Jesus is forced to carry his cross
to his crucifixion.

5. The Crucifixion

Jesus is nailed to the cross and dies.

## THE GLORIOUS MYSTERIES

1. The Resurrection

God the Father raises Jesus from the dead.

2. The Ascension

The risen Jesus remains among us for 40 days before he ascends to heaven. He promises the apostles he will send the Holy Spirit to baptize them and guide them after he is gone.

3. The Descent of the Holy Spirit

The Holy Spirit descends upon the apostles as Jesus promised.

4. The Assumption

After a long life of service to God, Mary dies peacefully, and her body and soul are carried to heaven.

5. The Coronation of Mary as Queen of Heaven

After she arrives in Paradise, Mary is crowned Queen of Heaven and Earth.

(And in later years I would add to my list the Luminous Mysterious introduced by Pope John Paul II, which, chronologically, come after the Joyful Mysteries.)

## THE LUMINOUS MYSTERIES

### 1. The Baptism of Jesus

John the Baptist baptizes Jesus in the River Jordan. God proclaims that Jesus is His beloved son.

### 2. The Wedding at Cana

After Jesus is baptized, he and Mary attend a wedding in Cana. At Mary's request, Jesus performs his first miracle, turning water into wine. Even though his mission hadn't started, Jesus performs the miracle out of love for his mother.

### 3. The Proclamation of the Kingdom

Jesus starts preaching; his mission will last three years, until he is crucified. Jesus calls all to conversion and service to the Kingdom of God.

### 4. The Transfiguration

As the time of his crucifixion nears, Jesus reveals his glory to Peter, James, and John.

### 5. The Institution of the Eucharist

At the Last Supper Jesus offers bread and wine to his disciples, telling them to remember him by this act, for the bread is his body and the wine is his blood.

So that was my list of Rosary Mysteries, a list that now made perfect sense to me. I still had a week before my big test, so I spent an hour each day going over everything I had studied.

I combined my Prayer List with my Mysteries List, jotted down all the how-to directions in my rosary notebook, and drew a little diagram of a rosary to show myself how to put everything together in anticipation of the day when I would finally pray a full rosary on my own.

Then, of course, I made another list so I'd have everything I'd learned in one place. I called that my Master List, and it looked like what I have illustrated on the following page.

# MASTER LIST ON HOW TO PRAY THE ROSARY

1. While holding the crucifix, make and say the Sign of the Cross and then recite the Apostles' Creed.

2. Recite the Our Father on the first bead.

3. Recite a Hail Mary on each of the next three beads.

4. Recite the Glory Be and the Fátima Prayer on the next bead, where we announce (or silently recall) the first mystery and then reflect upon it. Then, on the same bead, we say the Lord's Prayer.

5. On each of the next ten beads (the first decade!), recite a Hail Mary.

6. On the next single bead, recite the Glory Be and the Fátima Prayer.

7. Do the same on each decade, while remembering to announce the appropriate mystery. Reflect on the mysteries after saying the Glory Be and the Fátima Prayer, but before saying the Lord's Prayer.

8. When the final mystery is completed and we say the ten Hail Marys of the last decade, we finish praying the rosary by reciting the Glory Be, the Fátima Prayer, the Hail Holy Queen Prayer, and making the Sign of the Cross.

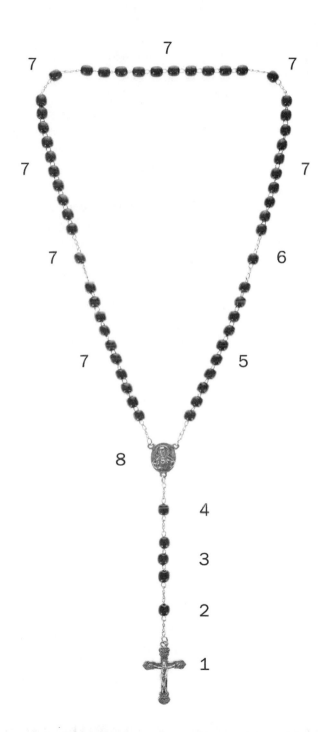

And that was it. I had done all the studying I could, I had prayed for help, I had picked the brains of the two most knowledgeable priests in our area, and I hadn't been without a rosary in my hand or in my pocket for weeks. I was ready to pray the rosary solo, and I found the perfect spot—on the edge of the steep hill at the far end of our backyard, overlooking the vast expanse of Lake Kivu, one of the largest lakes in Africa.

I waited until sunset and slipped outside so I could be alone for about a half hour. I found a comfortable place to sit by my mother's carefully tended rose garden, just as Lake Kivu became ablaze with the reflection of the descending sun.

I placed my fingers upon the crucifix dangling from my rosary, made the Sign of the Cross, beginning my first solo rosary prayer with these simple, amazing words:

*In the name of the Father, the Son, and the Holy Spirit. Amen.*

# CHAPTER 4

# THE ROSARY TEST

Despite how anxious I'd been in the weeks leading up to the big day, when the morning of my rosary test arrived I awoke with a huge grin on my face. I was surprisingly calm and happy, almost to the point of giddiness. My parents looked at me with bemused curiosity when I emerged from my bedroom and skipped out the back door, singing "Ave Maria" without a single complaint as I tackled my morning chores of gathering firewood, sweeping debris from the front walkway, and fetching fresh water from the spring down the hill.

It was only a 25-minute hike along the path to the bottom of the hill, but it took more than an hour for me to climb back up, since I had to lug two heavy buckets of water in either hand. I tried to hurry, though, because more than 100 children were signed up for the test and I didn't want to be the last in line.

The test was held only once a year. I had waited outside when both my older brothers had taken it, so I knew how panicky and agitated the kids standing in line could get. In Rwanda, at least for us Catholics, doing well in school and advancing through the various stages of our faith was a huge deal. There was enormous pressure to succeed placed on the shoulders of us students by our priests, nuns, parents, aunts, uncles, cousins, neighbors, and siblings. In my little town everyone knew how everyone else was doing, be it in work, school, business, or family affairs. How we performed in school or church studies reflected upon our families—so we all were expected to do our very best.

When we finished a school term, our teachers did not notify our parents about our scholastic progress by mailing a report card home. Oh no . . . when the term ended, every student in the district was lined up outside the school for a performance ceremony that the entire community could attend. The district principal would call out the name of each child, beckon him or her to step forward, and then loudly announce the rank that he or she had attained. My eldest brother, Aimable, was Student Number One every single year. I was always proud of him, but my heart was also with the kids who were publicly assigned the rank of Student 200 or 300 while their friends and families looked on with sadness and disappointment.

Passing the rosary test and the rest of the Confirmation testing was not a foregone conclusion—every year a significant percentage of kids were told to study harder and come back and try again the following year. Failing the test could impact your standing in Catholic school, which could affect if you passed or failed a grade or if you received a scholarship. It could perhaps even determine if you got into university or not. So yes, the pressure to succeed was daunting . . . and I always felt that it was tenfold for my brothers and me.

You see, my parents were the first in their families—and two of only a handful in our entire region—to have gone to university. They were both educators: my mom was a teacher at the village elementary school, and my dad was both a principal and a district superintendent responsible for schools throughout our province. What's more, Mom and Dad were well-known and respected leaders in the community, whose advice and counsel on all matters was sought out by people from every walk of life and for many miles around.

Even as our parents worked to ensure that we consistently met their high standard of excellence in academics and religious studies, they were never mean or overbearing with us kids. They didn't have to be. We never had to be told to do our homework, since we knew what was expected of us and just did it—two hours every day after school and several hours on the weekend.

Mom and Dad drilled two guiding principles into our heads from the moment we were born: The first was to be well educated, because education was the only way to rise out of the abject poverty that kept Rwanda and so much of Africa locked in a dehumanizing death grip. The second principle (and even more important one, they stressed) was to be a good and decent person, and the only sure way to accomplish that was to embrace and spread the love of God, to learn and understand the life lessons of the Bible, and to follow in the footsteps of Jesus as closely as humanly possible.

My parents' expectations bore fruit, as my two older brothers were both stellar academics and well-loved members of the community, and I was always one of the top students in my class.

ALTHOUGH I DID FEEL PRESSURE from all directions to earn near perfect marks on every test I ever took, I was feeling carefree and joyful on this lovely morning as I climbed the hill toward home. As I mentioned, my only concern was to arrive for the test before too many other students got there. Even so, I must have been daydreaming more than usual because it was much later than I thought when I reached the top of the hill. That meant I'd have to run the two miles to the church where the test was being held to be at the front of the line. *It doesn't matter,* I thought. *It feels like a day when nothing could go wrong.*

I was still singing at the top of my lungs when I returned to the house, gaily swinging the water buckets at my side as easily as though they were filled with air.

"Such confidence!" my father said with a smile. "Tell me, aren't you even a little bit nervous, Immaculée? There is an awful lot for you to remember and, depending on which priest gives you the test, you could be asked some pretty tough questions this morning."

Some of the self-assurance I had been floating on started to drain away from me. I bent down and placed the water buckets on the kitchen floor, and by the time I'd straightened up and turned to answer my father, anxiety had returned.

"Now that I think about it . . . I guess I am a bit nervous," I said softly. Even with all my studying, prayers, and newfound technique for recalling the events of the mysteries, doubt in my own abilities was creeping into my heart.

My mother instantly sensed my mood shift and placed an encouraging hand on my shoulder while chastising my father. "For heaven's sake, Leonard, don't frighten the girl."

"Of course not, Rose," he said, still smiling at me. "She's studied her heart out for this test and will do fine. I just meant, well . . . if she was a bit nervous, she might like a little something special for luck."

Dad reached into his pocket and withdrew a small hand-carved wooden box. As he handed it to me, I gave him a hug. I didn't even have to open the box—I knew it was one of his many treasured rosaries that he had collected over the years. He was fond of them yet readily gave them to people he cared for when he thought they could use a little extra help or protection. He always said it was best not to get too attached to any one particular rosary because "the rosary is not a piece of jewelry. It is a beautiful, living prayer that dwells within us and should travel directly from our heart to the heart of Our Blessed Mother."

Dad returned my hug and wished me well on the test. Mom kissed me on the head and told me to hurry up and get dressed or I'd miss the test and have to wait another year.

Half an hour later I was standing at the door of the church all alone; I was the only kid there and the first in line. An hour later there were dozens and dozens of jittery 12- and 13-year-olds lined up behind me, most of them wringing their hands, frantically looking at notes on little scraps of paper, or nervously twisting their hair into knots. Some were actually crouching in the dirt crying. We were such a fearful and worried lot that if we had been in America people passing by would have thought we were lining up to be inoculated with a long, painful needle— or perhaps about to be drafted into the army!

Behind me in line, I heard all sorts of murmuring and desperately phrased questions being asked in frenzied conversations like this:

"Tell me, I can't remember—in what mystery did Mary and Joseph lose track of little Jesus when they were traveling from Jerusalem to go back home to Bethlehem?"

"What? Wait, that's wrong . . . they got lost on the way back home to *Nazareth* . . . they lived in Nazareth."

"Not Bethlehem?"

"No. Jesus was born in Bethlehem, but he lived in Nazareth with Mary and Joseph."

"Oh . . . so what mystery does it happen in?"

"Jesus's birth?"

"No, when he got lost."

"I can't remember . . . he got lost and his parents were so upset, it must belong in the Sorrowful Mysteries."

"But then they found him, so it must be in the Joyful Mysteries!"

"I just don't know anymore."

"Me neither . . . "

Other than the last-minute cramming sessions, the main topic of conversation in line was about whom was the better priest to be tested by—Father Rwagema or Father Clement. Almost everyone agreed that Father Rwagema was preferable because, although he was deeply devout and loved Mary and Jesus with all his heart, he was considered more easygoing, soft-hearted, and forgiving when it came to passing students with a lot of wrong answers.

Father Clement, on the other hand, was seen by many as extremely pious. He was also a very learned and stern theologian with a reputation for being tough on students he considered academically lazy. I think that was all quite true, but I happened to know Father Clement well because he was a dear friend of my father's and a frequent visitor to our home. I'd long been able to see that beneath his serious façade beat a huge heart of pure kindness.

Even so, I still silently prayed that I'd be tested by Father Rwagema—Father Clement's "holiness" somehow made me nervous, and when I was nervous I lost all ability to concentrate.

A bell rang in the distance, and the church doors swung open. And there before me, sitting behind a long wooden table, sat Father Clement. He was writing something in a large notebook, and when he looked up at me his face was very somber and businesslike.

"Immaculée, the early bird," he said flatly. "Come in and shut the door behind you, please."

A MOMENT LATER I WAS STANDING In the center of the empty room, looking up at the ceiling one moment and then staring at my feet the next . . . anything to avoid making eye contact with Father Clement. As I had feared, he was making me very nervous. My mouth was dry, my hands were clammy, and I could feel rivulets of sweat running down my back. I reached into the pocket of my dress and squeezed the rosary Dad had just given to me.

"Let's begin, shall we?" Father Clement said in a very serious tone. "Immaculée, please answer this question: what is the third Joyful Mystery?"

I can't remember exactly what happened first, whether I let out a laugh before I did a little jump, or jumped first and then laughed. All I recall clearly is that the moment Father Clement asked me that first question, my heart became so light I thought I would float off the floor.

"Father Clement, the third Joyful Mystery is the Nativity! The third Joyful Mystery happens in a manger where the beautiful, kind, and loving Blessed Virgin Mary gives birth to her beloved son, Our Lord and Savior, the sweet baby Jesus. The story of the Nativity is found in the Gospel of Luke. It occurs after the Second Joyful Mystery, which is the Visitation, and before the fourth Joyful Mystery, which is the Presentation—"

"Very good, Immaculée," the priest broke in. "That's enough—it was one question, not three." He wrote something in his notebook and said, "Let's move on to the second question." But this time I thought I did see a hint of a smile in his eyes.

Father Clement asked me dozens of questions about the rosary, the mysteries, the sacraments, and many other aspects of my Catholic faith, all of which I answered as easily and joyously as I had the first. While talking to the venerable man of the cloth who, at least momentarily, held my fate in his hands, I felt as natural and relaxed as I would have been while talking to one of my girlfriends. It felt more like a conversation than a test, and it was the most pleasant conversation with an adult I'd had up to that point in my life.

The only regret or disappointment I felt was when I realized that Father Clement had gotten up and opened the door. The test was over.

"That's it?" I asked.

"That's it, my child. You can see there are many others waiting their turn."

"Did I do okay?"

"A perfect score . . . congratulations, Immaculée."

I walked out of the church with a sense of euphoria that lasted for an entire minute, which was as long as it took before I was mobbed by the throng of panicky preteen boys and girls waiting in line to be tested. I was swept up in a frantic inquisition demanding to know what questions I had been asked and what they could expect on the other side of the closed door. Most of the questions my frightened friends put to me concerned the same problem that had perplexed me: how to remember the events and the order of the mysteries.

I had become completely encircled, so I stepped up onto a little porch adjacent to the church door. I held my rosary above my head and raised my voice to reach as many of the kids as I could. "Let me tell you the trick I used to memorize the mysteries," I announced. "It is foolproof, and I can teach it to you before Father Clement opens that door again."

For the rest of the day I stood beside the church door tutoring small groups of worried youngsters as they moved through the line. I spent hours explaining how I had found it as difficult as everyone else to memorize the mysteries in an effective way, until I was inspired to think of them as groups of chronological events.

"Listen, guys, just think of it this way," I instructed. "Before our mothers gave birth to us, someone had to give them the good news that they were pregnant, right? Well, it is the same with Mary—and that is the first Joyful Mystery, the Annunciation! Then what comes next? Our moms were pregnant with us for nine months, and they visited friends and families during that time to share the good news . . . that is the second Joyful Mystery, the Visitation, when pregnant Mary visits her cousin Elizabeth. Then, of course, the third Joyful Mystery must be when Jesus is born: the Nativity!

"Don't you see how simple and logical it is? First the good news, then the pregnancy, then the baby is born— it makes sense. Do you understand? Jesus can't be lost or found in the temple if he is still a baby, can he? No! In the temple he is already a big boy! And he can't be whipped at the pillar after he is crucified, right? So just remember to always recall the events of the mysteries in chronological order, and you will never forget them again!"

Sighs of relief slowly replaced the looks of apprehension and distress I'd seen on so many of the young faces around me. Believe it or not, this one study tip for memorizing the mysteries proved to be so effective for me, and for the kids I shared it with that day, that I still teach it to people all over the world whenever I am discussing the rosary. Every single person I have shared my little trick with has thanked me profusely and said it made praying the rosary infinitely easier for them, which meant they prayed it more often, and reaped more of its benefits in the process.

And even on that particular testing day back in Rwanda some three decades ago, my study advice helped many of my schoolmates pass the test.

Father Clement saw me talking to different groups of children every time he opened the church door. When the testing was over, he said to me, "I'm not sure what you told all those kids, but we had fewer failures this year than any year I can remember. Maybe you should become a teacher one day . . . that is, if you have given up the idea of becoming a nun." This was his way of teasing me about the day months earlier when I had shown up at his parish with my best friend pleading to be sent to a nunnery so that we could devote our lives to God and the Blessed Mother. The wise priest's response had been to tell us to go away and think it over for a couple years.

I took Father Clement's advice. As fate would have it, I did not become a nun—but in a way, I did become a teacher. The one lesson I have to offer is how the power of God's love and forgiveness can transform our hearts and our world, and one of the greatest ways to access that divine power is through praying the rosary.

# CHAPTER 5

# PROMISES, PROMISES

After passing my rosary test the world seemed to open up before me. It was a happy, heady, and wonderful time. Passing the test meant that I could be confirmed in the Catholic Church, which I soon was, marking my full entrance into the faith. On that day I stood before God and my family and promised to follow in the footsteps of Christ.

Not long after that I marked another milestone in my life, my 13th birthday and entrance into young womanhood. It wouldn't be long before I'd be moving away from home to attend high school.

I HAD ALWAYS WORKED HARD and maintained one of the highest grade averages in the district, so everyone assumed I would be accepted into the best girls' high school in Rwanda, Lycée de Notre Dame d'Afrique, with a full scholarship. Lycée was almost a day's journey by bus from home, but was the only choice of high school for any female student aspiring to attend university. The faculty's academic standards were so highly respected that the president of the country sent his daughter there. Another huge plus of attending Lycée was that my dear brother Damascene was studying at a seminary less than half a mile away. That meant he could keep an eye on me for Dad, while also keeping me company.

Attending Lycée had been a dream of mine throughout grade school because my heart was set on attending university and majoring in math and science. But my dreams were dashed by the bigoted policies of Rwanda's racist government.

As I have written about at length in *Left to Tell,* when I was growing up Rwanda was ruled by an extremist Hutu government that enforced increasingly racist, anti-Tutsi laws. Tutsis were prohibited from holding government or university jobs, and thousands of Tutsi children were denied attendance at good, fully funded public schools like Lycée. By the time I'd reached high-school age, a student's marks no longer mattered when it came to school placement: the law stated that 85 percent of public-school seats must be filled with Hutu students, because 85 percent of Rwandans were Hutus.

A month before the school year started I was notified that my application to Lycée had been rejected. There was no point in applying to any other public schools because all vacant seats had been assigned to Hutus or the handful of Tutsi children whose parents were rich. The news meant I would never go to university—and in Rwandan society, that meant the furthest I would go professionally was the position of housewife.

I locked myself away in my room and cried for two days. I was so self-absorbed in my personal tragedy that it didn't even occur to me to pray for help or guidance, nor did I think about how my parents were feeling about the situation. They had pushed me since kindergarten to succeed at school so that I could earn a master's degree or a doctorate, and their dreams for me had been crushed as well. When I finally went to ask them how they were feeling, I discovered my dad had sold two of our cows (the equivalent of three years' wages) to buy me a placement in a private high school four hours away from home.

"But it's too expensive," I protested, even though I was overjoyed by their love and generosity.

"You worry about your studies, dear," my mother told me, wiping a tear from my cheek. "Let your father worry about everything else."

As he drove me to the distant village where I'd spend the next two years studying, Dad told me to remember my faith and the promise I had made on my confirmation day: to follow in the footsteps of Jesus. Dad had always protected me from Rwanda's rampant racism. He and Mom had also raised me in an atmosphere of Christian love and tolerance; it broke his heart to see me suffering because of the actions and dictates of evil men.

"There are demons in this world, Immaculée, some are visible and some hide in men's hearts," Dad said during the long drive. Then he slid another little wooden box across the seat to me, another rosary gift on another important occasion in my life. "Protect your faith and never give up hope. Remember to pray the rosary and ask for the Blessed Mother's help—she will always be with you in your hour of need."

Much to my surprise, my new school was a Protestant academy run by Seventh-day Adventists. The faculty mostly consisted of transient teachers from Rwanda or the Congo (back then it was called Zaire), and they moved around a lot from school to school. There was no running water, the electricity was spotty, and our dorm room was a rectangular cinder-block cell with a few dozen thin mattresses lining the concrete floor. It wasn't the famous Lycée, with its European faculty and beautiful grounds, but it *was* a high school—and my parents had spent everything they had to get me enrolled. I vowed to get even higher marks than I usually did so that I would make Mom and Dad proud of me.

I FOLLOWED MY FATHER'S ADVICE and tried to keep my faith strong by praying every day, but praying my rosary became the greatest challenge of my new academic life. Seventh-day Adventists I have met over the years believe in religious freedom and tolerance, but the directors of my school were not like that. They may not have been openly anti-Catholic, but they did make it clear that you were doomed if you didn't believe what they believed. We had to observe the Sabbath on Saturday and attend services on Friday night.

I loved the sermons and the passion with which they were delivered. Yet I often felt intimidated when the preacher, who was usually a professor or school director, shouted out for everyone who wanted their souls to be saved to get up and stand beside him. There were several occasions when my Catholic friend Beatrice—who would rather die than be saved by a Protestant—and I would be left sitting by ourselves while the entire school assembly stared back at us with self-righteous pity from the front of the room, as though they were on their way to heaven and we were going straight to hell.

I respected their beliefs but held on to my faith as tightly as I held on to the rosary I kept hidden in my pocket. It felt too uncomfortable for me to take my beads out and pray openly, but sometimes at night I would sit with the few other Catholic girls in our darkened dorm room, discussing the visionaries of Kibeho and how the Virgin Mother continually pleaded for everyone to pray the rosary. Many people had been horribly frightened when Our Lady presented the seers with images of Rwanda overflowing in a river of blood, burned-out homes, and the remains of dismembered corpses strewn across the landscape. We all shivered as we pictured the horrid images in our own minds.

"It was a warning," one of my schoolmates whispered. "Mary said many Rwandans secretly hate their neighbors, and unless everyone prays the rosary to remove hatred from their hearts, our country will drown in our own blood."

"She didn't say that," another one said. "Mary is sweet and gentle; she would never show such ugly things."

"But she did," I said, as upset as they were. I recalled the terror in the seers' voices the day their visions had been broadcast on the radio. "Alphonsine, Anathalie, and Marie-Claire were crying and begging Mary to stop showing them such horrible things. Our priest Father Rwagema was there, and he said that some of the people listening to the visionaries were driven mad. He said Mary warned us that a great terror would destroy Rwanda unless we all prayed the rosary and started loving each other."

It's remarkable to me today that, although I heard Mary's warnings over and over again, I never connected them to the hateful, racist polices in Rwanda—policies that had brought me to that very school in the first place! Mary told us that a genocide was coming, it was obvious to see, and all we had to do was pray the rosary to stop it—but we didn't.

Although my rosary praying fell off quite a bit while at the Seventh-day Adventist school, my marks were better than ever. But it was always such a relief to come home on holidays. Not only could I catch up with friends and family, but I could pray openly without fear of being censured or chastised.

During those home visits I loved meeting up with girlfriends to spend a wild Friday night praying the rosary together—there wasn't much nightlife in my little village! However, we grew bored constantly repeating the Hail Mary, so one evening we started singing the rosary. There are many beautiful Rwandan songs celebrating the mysteries and we learned them all. Suddenly, instead of mumbling *Hail Mary* we began harmonizing and singing *Ave Maria*. Singing to our Blessed Mother made us feel so good we simply had to get to our feet and dance.

Our Friday rosary outings became such joyous worship sessions that soon kids from other villages were walking for miles to come pray with us. To this day one of my favorite ways to worship and celebrate God and Mary is to dance and sing the beautiful prayers of the rosary.

The only thing amiss during my visits home was that my father sometimes seemed distant or distracted. After evening prayers he disappeared into his room for the night, which was highly unusual. Dad always loved gathering the family together after dinner and listening to each of us recount our days, but now he spent more and more time alone. Sometimes I'd see him at the far end of our yard staring out across Lake Kivu for hours at a time. Mom assured me that everything was fine; Dad just had a lot to think about in his work. But I soon discovered that he was spending time alone for an entirely different reason.

TWO YEARS AFTER LYCÉE REJECTED ME I was invited to retake the entrance exam. Many Hutu students who'd been automatically placed in the school had flunked out, and the school had to fill the seats to keep European grant money coming in. But the government's anti-Tutsi policies had only grown more cruel and intolerant, so I was certain

I would be rejected again. Still, I had promised my father I would keep my faith and not despair, so I took the exam.

I was at home when the news came: I had achieved a nearly perfect score on the exam and was accepted into Lycée with a full scholarship! Everyone in the family went crazy—Mom was crying, Damascene was dancing, Dad was shouting thanks to God for answering two years of prayers. The rest of us didn't understand what Dad meant, but that didn't stop us from celebrating together all evening.

My father took me aside later and explained that he'd been praying the rosary every single day since I was first rejected by Lycée. He pleaded with Mary to "intercede" on his behalf, in order to help me get into the school I deserved to go to and that everyone wanted me to attend.

"What do you mean, you asked Mary to intercede?" I replied, suddenly realizing that whenever he'd slipped away from the family over the past two years, he'd been going to pray the rosary for me! I was again touched by his deep love for me, but still confused by what he meant when he prayed for Mary to intercede on his behalf.

"I asked her to talk to Jesus for me. That's what the Blessed Mother tells us to do every time she appears somewhere—she tells us we can ask her for whatever we want, and promises she will take our requests straight to her son. Then she prays for us like any good mother prays for her child. Jesus is the Lord, after all. He's the one who gets things done, but it's best to get Mary on your side. Jesus loves her so much that he just can't say no to her."

I laughed to hear my father talk about the Holy Family with such familiarity; he was always quite formal when discussing religion, but he loved Mary as much as I did—maybe even more. Still, I was confused.

"Dad, I just don't get it . . . I don't understand why you asked Mary for a favor. I mean, I always pray for her and Jesus and God to protect our family, but I wouldn't dare ask for a personal favor as big as getting me into a school. Isn't it against the rules? Aren't we just supposed to pray for other people and not for ourselves?"

"Of course not!" he answered. "In the promises she gave to St. Dominic she tells us she will give us whatever we want, as long as we pray from the heart for something we truly need."

"What promises are you talking about?"

"The 15 promises she gave to St. Dominic when she presented him with the rosary back in the Middle Ages." My father shook his head and tsk-tsked at my blank expression, then started walking toward the village, beckoning for me to follow. "I honestly don't know how you scored so highly on your rosary test without knowing what the 15 promises of the rosary are."

We walked together for a quarter of a mile until we reached the little rosary chapel he had built a few months after Mary first appeared in Rwanda. The chapel was his gift to Our Lady so that our neighbors and pilgrims to Kibeho could sit in peace and pray their beads.

It was a simple little room furnished with one wooden bench. The only decorations were three sheets of paper tacked onto the bare wooden walls. One sheet had directions for praying the traditional Catholic rosary, the second sheet had directions on how to pray the Rosary of the Seven Sorrows (which Mary encouraged us to pray in Kibeho, and I included in my book *Our Lady of Kibeho*), and the third sheet is reprinted on the next page. Dad and I stood there in silence and read Mary's promises together.

## THE 15 PROMISES OF MARY

1.  To all those who recite my rosary devoutly, I promise my special protection and very great graces.

2.  Those who will persevere in the recitation of my rosary shall receive some signal grace.

3.  The rosary shall be a very powerful armor against hell; it shall destroy vice, deliver from sin, and dispel heresy.

4.  The rosary shall make virtue and good works flourish, and shall obtain for souls the most abundant divine mercies; it shall substitute in hearts love of God for love of the world, elevate them to desire heavenly and eternal goods. Oh, that souls would sanctify themselves by this means!

5.  Those who trust themselves to me through the rosary shall not perish.

6.  Those who will recite my rosary piously, considering its mysteries, shall not be overwhelmed by misfortune nor die a bad death. The sinner shall be converted; the just shall grow in grace and become worthy of eternal life.

7.  Those truly devoted to my rosary shall not die without the consolations of the Church, or without grace.

8.  Those who will recite my rosary shall find during their life and at their death the light of God, the fullness of His grace, and shall share in the merits of the blessed.

9. I will deliver very promptly from purgatory the souls devoted to my rosary.

10. The true children of my rosary shall enjoy great glory in heaven.

11. What you ask through my rosary, you shall obtain.

12. Those who propagate my rosary shall obtain through me aid in all their necessities.

13. I have obtained from my son that all the advocates of the rosary shall have for intercessors the entire celestial court during their life and at the hour of death.

14. Those who recite my rosary faithfully are all my beloved children, the brothers and sisters of Jesus Christ.

15. Devotion to my rosary is a special sign of predestination

When we finished reading, my father turned to me and said, "You see, she promises to give us whatever we ask for when we pray the rosary—but she promises so much more."

"I can't believe I never knew about this." I sighed and laughed at the same time. "I had no idea I could pray for personal things . . . and I can't believe I have another rosary list to memorize!"

# CHAPTER 6

# ROSARY ROAD TRIP

It took the Blessed Mother two years to answer Dad's daily rosary prayers and get me into Lycée, so we didn't waste any time putting the miracle into motion. The day after celebrating my acceptance, I packed my few belongings into the trunk of the family car, kissed my teary-eyed mother good-bye, hopped into the front seat next to my father, and set off on the four-hour drive to my new life at my new school. My brother Damascene was along for the ride and comfortably stretched out across the backseat.

For the first half hour of the trip my brother, who was the sweetest boy I have ever known, delighted in teasing me for not knowing about the 15 promises of Mary. When Dad showed me the promises for the first time the previous night, I'd found the language to be extremely old-fashioned and confusing—but always the obsessive student, I copied the list to study later. I was wishing I'd studied it before climbing into the car with Damascene. We were very competitive siblings when it came to studying, no matter what the topic.

"So tell me, little sister," he said, echoing our father's chastisement from the night before. "How did you manage to pull off a perfect score on the rosary test without having a clue what the 15 promises are?"

I turned around to argue with him, but he was flashing that beautiful smile of his that just seemed to say "I love you, Immaculée." It melted my heart every time. I smiled back at him and confessed that I didn't understand the promises. I took a look at my list and shrugged— I was baffled!

"Number 13 sounds so strange: *I have obtained from my son that all the advocates of the rosary shall have for intercessors the entire celestial court during their life and at the hour of death.* I don't want to sound ignorant, but I don't have any idea what a celestial court is. Damascene, have you studied it in the seminary?"

He smiled at me again and said, "The celestial court is where the angels play basketball in heaven." I laughed at his dumb joke, probably because he laughed at it first. I always loved how my brother found his jokes funnier than anyone else did. Only a couple of years earlier I would have believed him and started asking my priests and teachers what their favorite celestial-court basketball team was. Damascene was so likeable and good-natured that I was willing to believe everything he said.

Even our father chuckled at Damascene's joke, and Dad never kidded when it came to religion, especially about anything concerning Mary or the rosary. He hadn't said much up until now because so much of the long trip through Rwanda's hilly landscape involved negotiating hairpin turns and avoiding 200-foot drop-offs. But the conversation was too inviting for a rosary devotee like Dad to miss.

"All joking aside, Immaculée," he began, "what Mary's 13th promise means is that everyone who prays and encourages others to pray the rosary will be watched over throughout their entire life by all the angels in heaven . . . and when we die, angels will be there to meet us and escort us through the gates of heaven. The Blessed Mother herself will be waiting to welcome us home." Dad's voice had grown soft; he was smiling to himself and had a misty look in his eyes. It was rare for my reserved father to get emotional, so even this tiny flicker of sweet sentimentality spoke volumes about his affection for Mary.

Damascene and I exchanged glances and smiled at each other. For a few long moments no one said a word, and then Dad reverted to his didactic school-principal mode. I knew our lecture on the 15 promises was about to commence.

"The term *celestial court* refers to the heavenly host; basically, it means everyone who lives in heaven and worships God. A king on Earth has a royal court, and the King of Heaven has a celestial court. It is important not to get bogged down in the old-fashioned language while reading the promises or the prayers of the rosary—or even some versions of the Bible, for that matter. When language gets between us and God, we are the ones who miss out," Dad explained. "Find the heart of what the words are telling you . . . you must feel the words of Jesus and Mary in your heart, or you will never be able to follow in their footsteps."

I read the 15 promises aloud, and both my father and brother shared their thoughts and feelings about them with me. We marveled at the magnitude of the guarantees found on that heavenly list. The promises assure us that if we pray the rosary correctly it will multiply the effects of the good deeds we do, help turn other people away from greed and hatred while making them loving and kind, and usher the souls of our departed loved ones into heaven more quickly.

"The rosary is the greatest untapped power source on the planet," Dad said. "Just think of what the world would be like if armies fought each other with rosaries instead of guns . . . there would be peace on Earth within a day."

At that moment he swerved to avoid a convoy of military transport trucks carrying government soldiers. We had seen a lot of troop movement on the narrow roadway as we neared the Ugandan border. Many Tutsis forced into exile had formed a rebel army in our neighboring country. They were trying to force the Rwandan president to give the persecuted Tutsi minority protection and equal rights. There had been fighting between the Hutu army and Tutsi rebels along the border, and there were rumors of civil war.

My father was a great believer in peaceful negotiation and that people were basically good. He had suffered discrimination and persecution at the hands of his jealous Hutu colleagues for years, but he'd rather turn the other cheek than harm another person. My brothers were more suspicious of our fellow Rwandans, especially when they heard government officials publicly calling for Tutsi "cockroaches" like my family to be exterminated. Tutsis were being dehumanized and demonized every day on the radio, but life went on for us. Dad, as I've said before, had protected me from the ugly ethnic hatred that surrounded us and raised us to treat everyone with kindness and respect.

"I hope we don't get pulled over and asked to show our identity cards," Damascene said with genuine concern.

"We've done nothing wrong. They have no reason to bother us."

"I hope that's true, Dad. People who live in this part of the country don't like people like us, they don't like

Tutsis. But you don't have to worry, Immaculée. Like I told you before, your school has a giant fence and excellent security—it's the safest place in the region."

Several other military trucks rumbled by, and Damascene added: "But a little protection couldn't hurt, so remember the first promise on your list: *To all those who recite my rosary devoutly, I promise my special protection and very great graces.*"

WHEN WE REACHED THE NORTHERN SHORE of Lake Kivu, we stopped to eat the lunch Mom had packed for us. The lake seemed to stretch out forever before melting into the horizon. I looked out on the vast sparkling blue waters, the same waters that many miles to the south lapped against the shoreline beneath our home. I remembered praying my first "solo" rosary sitting on the edge of the hill in the backyard overlooking that shoreline, and then I pictured Dad standing in that same spot in our yard every evening for two years, praying his rosary so that Mary would get me into the school I was now about to enter. Dad must have been thinking the same thing because he told me to never forget that we were here because of the rosary.

I told him I never would, and thanked him for his love and faith and for teaching me how to use the rosary to help with my personal needs. Realizing I could apply the power of the rosary to my own life was a major step forward in the journey of faith I began as a child.

"Promise number 11 is what you have to remember to help you at school," Damascene said, as though reading my thoughts. "*What you ask through my rosary, you shall obtain.* I have never taken an exam or written a test without reflecting on that promise and praying ten Hail Marys beforehand."

Other than our eldest brother, Aimable, Damascene was the most brilliant student I knew. I thanked him for the study tip, which I've used for every major test in and out of school ever since.

"Let's pray the rosary one more time together as a family before we drop you off at the school," Dad said. "We might not see each other for weeks, and there isn't a better way to thank Mary for the miracle she has just performed for us."

We all took out our separate rosaries and knelt together in a semicircle beneath a large shade tree on the shore of that beautiful lake. I couldn't have imagined a more perfect way to begin this new chapter in my life.

CHAPTER 7

# PERSONAL
# EMPOWERMENT

Lycée de Notre Dame d'Afrique was every bit as wonderful as I had dreamed. The teachers were incredibly gifted, the grounds were immaculate, and the science department was state of the art—and the nuns and priests were wonderfully strict in an old-world Catholic way, which compelled every girl to follow the rules to the letter and strive to do her absolute best.

There were no boys or other worldly pursuits to distract us. Daily Mass was mandatory, except on Sunday, when we went twice. It was perfect for me! I was homesick, but made some friends and saw Damascene when possible. Because of strict visitor regulations he could only come to campus twice a month. But we got around the rules by finding a spot along the high security fence where we could meet and chat, even if electrified wire hung between us.

I regularly employed my brother's pre-exam routine and prayed the rosary before every quiz and test, always remembering Our Lady's 11th rosary promise that with sincere prayer we can receive anything we ask for. My marks got higher with each exam, and my teachers and parents couldn't have been more pleased.

As time went by I expanded my requests, using the rosary to bring peace between myself and another student I had been squabbling with due to a misunderstanding. Our feud was ongoing for weeks, and she was bad-mouthing me to other girls. Her anger caused me pain, so I prayed the rosary asking Our Lady to intercede to bring peace between the other girl and me.

The next morning I opened my eyes to find my school-mate hovering above my face. I was frightened at first but then saw a tear in her eye. "I'm so sorry, Immaculée. I realized last night that this silly fight is entirely my fault. Can you forgive me, and can we be friends again?" I told her there was nothing to forgive, and we became as close as sisters. Not only that, but the girl privately went to each person to whom she had spoken ill of me and apologized for slandering me with untruths.

I was constantly amazed by how I could use the rosary to bring small miracles into my life. At one point I grew concerned that the beads might become too much of a temptation and feared I could be drawn into praying for things I shouldn't pray for—a large sum of money, super-expensive fashions, or an important job I wasn't qualified for.

Worry about potential abuse drove me to one of our school priests. He smiled when I confessed my fears and assured me I had nothing to worry about. "Child, you are fretting about the impossible," he said comfortingly. "To begin with, do you think God would answer any prayer that could cause us harm? No . . . that will never happen. Second, remember that the key to the power of the rosary is sincerity. Without sincerity, prayers are as powerless as they are meaningless. And here is the crucial point—an open, honest heart will never ask for something it knows it does not need or deserve. If your prayers are sincere, you will ask only for what you truly need."

I was so impressed and enlightened that my jaw must have dropped, and he began to laugh. "Okay, Immaculée, off you go," he said through his chuckles. "Problem solved! See you at your next confession."

With priestly reassurance that I would not abuse the beads and pray the rosary with anything but the purest of intentions, I decided to ask Mary to help me meet a boy I had a secret crush on. My designs were strictly chaste, of course, but my schoolgirl heart skipped a beat every time I thought of him. *Who knows,* I told myself. *One day after I earn my Ph.D., he may end up being Mr. Right.*

His name was Pierre, and he grew up in the town neighbouring my home village. He was tall and very handsome, funny and athletic, and had (with the exception of Damascene) the nicest smile I'd ever seen. We had glanced shyly at each other at church socials, soccer games, and even at the rosary prayer groups my friends and I had started where everyone sang and danced while praising the Blessed Mother. I think I was a little bit in love with him since I was 12 or 13, but as my mother and father made it clear they wouldn't let me start dating until I was middle-aged, I kept my puppy-love infatuation to myself.

Pierre certainly didn't have a clue as to how I felt about him. I didn't even dare tell my best friend, Janet, about my crush for fear she might accidently let it slip, and then he'd find out . . . and then everyone else would find out . . . and then I'd surely die from embarrassment.

At any rate, I happened to know, through a friend of a friend of his sister, that he was going away to a new boarding school the same day I was arriving back home for a midterm holiday. According to the schedule I had been studying for over a week, if I left on the early-morning bus and Pierre arrived at the central station near our homes to catch the last afternoon bus that would take him to his new school, we would be on the same platform for exactly half an hour. And if that happened to be the case, I was certain that I might accidently bump into him—and then, who knows, he might even say "Hi" to me.

However, there were several buses he could leave town on that day, and most of them left before I would arrive. So a few days before I was to leave for home I began praying the rosary and asking Mary to arrange for everything to happen the way it must in order for Pierre and me to meet on the bus platform. I thanked her in advance, because I knew she would not deny me such an important favor, especially if she felt such a meeting was the right thing to happen at that point in time for both this young man and myself.

I chuckle now thinking back on this teenaged prayer, but because of its sweetness, not because I think it is silly. I have seen so much heartache, loneliness, and sorrow in the lives of people I've met since the genocide that I believe with utter conviction that one of the greatest usages of prayer, particularly the rosary prayer, is to seek peace and healing for a broken or heavy heart—whether that heart beats in the chest of a 15-year-old girl or of a 105-year-old great-great-grandmother. I believe God is love and the more love we have in our lives, the closer our lives will be to God.

WHEN THE DAY I WAS SURE I WAS DESTINED to meet Pierre finally arrived, the bus that would take me to him showed up at Lycée 12 minutes behind schedule. The bus journey was hours longer than the same trip made by car, and every second counted. I had already lost 12 precious minutes with Pierre before I'd climbed onto the bus and taken my seat.

The trip was torture for me. We were stopped by the military, who searched the bus for rebels, then were detained by a shepherd driving goats across the road. There was a rockslide that had to be cleared, a fallen tree that had to be rolled to the shoulder, and a flat tire that took an hour to repair.

Nevertheless, I prayed the rosary the entire journey, asking Mary to make this little miracle come true and thanking her even if it didn't because she'd given me so many wonderful gifts already. By the time we arrived at the central bus station, the sun was setting and I knew that Pierre was long gone—the last bus he could possibly have taken had left the station more than four hours earlier. As my bus turned to enter the station I stood up to get my bag and tucked my rosary into my pocket. At that moment the bus jolted to a stop to let another vehicle pass in front and I banged against the window.

My nose was pressed against the glass and my eyes were as wide as golf balls. Six inches away from my face sat Pierre, on a bus that was slowly passing by ours. He spotted me a moment after I saw him. His face exploded with a dazzling smile, and he jumped from his seat and pulled down his window. I immediately did the same, and we each reached an arm out to the other and clasped hands. Our fingers entwined for only a few seconds as our eyes locked onto each other, and in the same instant we silently said hello and farewell.

A moment later his bus lurched into traffic and our fingers slipped apart. He stuck his head out the window, smiled at me once more, and literally drove off into the sunset. That was the last time I ever saw this beautiful boy—

a few years later he would be hacked to death with machetes wielded by young men he had called friends his entire life.

Pierre died without ever knowing how I felt about him, but thanks to the Blessed Virgin Mary and the power of the rosary we had a sweet and tender moment that I have kept alive and treasured in a corner of my heart for more than two decades.

AFTER MEETING PIERRE LIKE THAT, against all odds and despite common sense, I developed even greater faith in Mary's promises. My life got just a little bit sweeter whenever I prayed with the beads. When the time came to write my entrance exam for the National University in Butare, I prayed the rosary every day for a month, asking for the Blessed Mother to help me and my three best friends be accepted by the very tough-to-get-into university science program.

When the acceptance notices were posted on the cafeteria wall, the screams that erupted created a minor security alert. The entire senior science class was accepted en masse into the same prestigious university program, which was a first in the history of the school.

My life seemed perfect. I spent two years studying at a wonderful university in the field of my choice and was roommates with my best friend from high school. During that time, I also met a boy I liked who loved Jesus and accompanied me to Bible study and gospel sing-alongs. In addition, it looked as though I was going to be accepted into a graduate program and would earn a master's degree like my brother Damascene—and just maybe, I'd start working on a doctorate, as my brother Aimable was doing in faraway Senegal. Most important, my prayer life was full and rewarding. I was confident that if I continued to pray the rosary, I would always be happy, and life would just get better and better.

I only wish that many more Rwandans had felt the same way about the rosary—but they didn't.

The Virgin Mary had warned us 12 years earlier that if we didn't pray for God to fill our hearts with love, a day would soon arrive that would bring a storm of blood and death to our land, the likes of which had never been seen before.

That day arrived on April 7, 1994.

———

# CHAPTER 8

# CARRYING MY ROSARY INTO HIDING

Once again, I was back in the loving comfort of my home. It was the Easter holidays, but my brother Aimable was still studying in Senegal, so I knelt for evening prayers with my parents and brothers Damascene and Vianney at my side. The warmth of our simple family tradition enveloped me, and I felt safe and protected; our love for each other and our mutual love of God was still strong and sustaining. The bonds that held our happy family together hadn't changed in the years I had been away at school, but everything around us had.

Our world started crashing down around us a few days after I arrived home. President Juvénal Habyarimana, who had promised peace and equality for all Rwandans, was murdered—his plane shot out of the sky on the say-so of government leaders who had long been plotting the genocide. At its core, the plan of the extremist Hutu politicians and military men was simple: arm every Hutu in the country with a machete and order them to kill every Tutsi they knew, or be executed themselves. The plan was as effective as it was diabolical.

The army, the police, and a drug-fueled hooligan militia was dispatched to take the lead in the killing, and to ensure that regular Hutu citizens had machetes and used them to murder their neighbors. The goal was to exterminate all 1.2 million Tutsis in Rwanda—to the last man, woman, and child. They had almost finished the job by the time they were chased out of the country a few months after the first Tutsi was murdered.

In our part of the country the screaming began within 24 hours of President Habyarimana's assassination. Hundreds and then thousands of Tutsis from across the region arrived on our doorstep, many maimed and seriously wounded, almost all of them in shock. As I've mentioned, my mother and father were respected and loved community leaders whom people turned to in times of need, and their need had never been greater. The accounts I heard of sadistic torture, dismemberment, murder, and rape will haunt me as long as I live.

I HAVE WRITTEN EXTENSIVELY about the first days of the genocide and its bleak aftermath in *Left to Tell* and *Led By Faith,* so I won't recount that dreadful time in detail here other than to show you how I came by the rosary I carried with me into hiding.

Our house and surrounding fields were transformed into a makeshift refugee camp, and my father was tacitly elected as leader and protector of the displaced thousands huddled in front of our home. As the sun rose on the second or third day of the horrible new reality, I spotted my father walking among the frightened families who crouched for warmth around the countless campfires burning in our cow pasture. He carried his favorite red-and-white rosary in his hand as he moved from family to family, offering words and prayers of encouragement.

At one point he scrambled atop a large boulder and called out to the multitude. "Friends," he boomed, his hands high above his head, the rosary glinting in the morning sun. "Do not fear these killers. They are not stronger than we are, not if we have God's love in our hearts. If they are acting out of evil, if they have come to harm us for no reason other than their hatred for us, then we will defeat them. Love will always conquer hatred. Believe in yourselves, believe in each other, and believe in God! Be strong; do not let fear cripple your faith.

"If this is the work of a gang of thugs, we will defeat them. But if this is part of a government conspiracy to eliminate Tutsis, we must accept that we are about to die—we cannot stop guns and grenades with sticks and stones. We should not be fearful; God has given us this time to prepare our hearts to enter heaven. Let us use this time to repent. Let us pray for our sins to be forgiven," Dad cried, raising his rosary aloft in his right hand and picking up a spear in his left. "If we are to die, let us die with our hearts clean. We will fight against this evil that has come to our homes, but we must not kill any of them, no matter what they do to us. We will enter heaven with no blood on our hands!"

Then he knelt upon the boulder and led the thousands of men, women, and children—most of whom were about to be slaughtered—through the comforting words of the Lord's Prayer. I still get goose bumps thinking about how many souls he helped to heaven that day by urging them to repent their sins while they still had time.

The killers attacked not long after that, and Dad ordered me to leave our home and seek shelter with our neighbor Pastor Murinzi. Although the pastor was a Hutu, he was also a longtime family friend whom my father was certain would protect me.

Before I left, Dad placed his red-and-white rosary into the palm of my hand. It was a farewell gift, and I feel that in giving it to me he was trying to say: "You don't have me to turn to anymore. From now on, this rosary is your father. Whenever you are in trouble, use it to call for help and help will come."

My father then ran out to fight the killers, and I was soon running as fast as my feet would carry me toward the house of our neighbor.

PASTOR MURINZI WELCOMED ME into his home. He had guests, some of whom were lifelong friends of mine, but who now treated me as though I was a cockroach because of my Tutsi blood. He quickly ushered me away from his guests and I waited in another part of the house to see what would happen.

As the hours ticked by, Damascene and my younger brother, Vianney, came to the pastor's home. Damascene told me that the killers had burned our house down, and that my parents had climbed onto Dad's motorcycle and just barely escaped with their lives. Then Damascene left to hide at a friend's house, leaving me in charge of Vianney.

Pastor Murinzi was a good man who agreed to hide seven other Tutsi women besides myself—but he made me tell Vianney that he had to leave because hiding a man was too dangerous. It was the most difficult decision of my life, but I was forced to say good-bye to my little brother. Then the pastor led me and the other women to the tiny three-foot-by-four-foot bathroom in the back of his bedroom. We all crammed in against each other, barely able to sit down or even breathe in the claustrophobic space that would be our home for the next three months while the killing raged on outside.

The pastor trusted no one and kept us safe by concealing our presence from everyone, even his own children. We were not allowed to speak, could flush the toilet only when another one in the house was flushed, and were mainly fed scraps from the garbage that wouldn't be missed.

Outside, and often inside the house itself, gangs of killers searched and hunted relentlessly for Tutsis they could murder, torture, and rape. The only hope of survival for the other women and myself was to sit in silence on top of one another in the sweltering, fetid confines of the tiny bathroom and hope that somehow the situation would improve.

And that was to be our life for the next three months.

Once again, I remind readers that I've already written about the 91 days I spent in the bathroom in painstaking detail. This book is not intended to provide a matching chronological account of what I have written before, but rather to explore anew the way prayer, particularly the prayers of the rosary, preserved my sanity and my soul during the darkest days of my life. More than anything, I want to show you how I learned a method of prayer that allowed me to communicate with God at a level and with a depth I had never imagined possible.

In the years since the genocide I've realized that it was the extraordinary events I was forced into that led me to this new form of praying—which, had I not been confronted with near-certain death every waking hour, I otherwise may not have found. Learning to pray the rosary as I did absolutely saved my life during the genocide. Yet, as I have delightedly stated before, it's also given me a life beyond my wildest dreams.

While I may have learned the great power of the rosary prayer during a nightmare I would not wish on any living soul, I know for a fact that we do not have to be facing danger or death for Our Lady to hear our cries, for Jesus to come to our aid, or for God to answer our prayers. They are always there for us, but by learning to travel toward them through more focused and profound prayer, we are able to meet them at ever-deepening depths within our own hearts. And that is where the rewards of prayer in our life become limitless.

Having said that, it was during the terrorizing early days of hiding in Pastor Murinzi's bathroom when I first sensed I was on the verge of discovering something remarkable: the existence of a higher plane of prayer that I had never been completely unaware of, but that I now felt was within my grasp. So let's step back there for a moment.

Within my first week in hiding, hundreds of Hutu killers amassed in the pastor's backyard on the other side of the bathroom wall. Some dressed like jungle savages, in animal skins with horns on their heads; all of them carried blood-stained spears, clubs, or machetes and sang hunting songs celebrating the murders of Tutsi women and babies.

Through a small bathroom window I recognized boys I had gone to school with and neighbors who'd been welcomed guests in my parents' home. Now they hunted me—even calling out my name, taunting me, singing for me to "come out, come out" from wherever I was because I couldn't hide forever. Somebody had said they'd seen me in the area, but I knew they weren't sure exactly where I was or I'd already be dead.

That's when the devil began whispering in my ear, tempting me to abandon hope, to scream out as loudly as I could to let the killers know where I was hiding, thus ending my fear and misery in one swoop of a machete blade.

Satan's voice was no illusion; I was not hallucinating or delusional. I could hear his voice as clearly as I could hear the killers' taunts. The devil was beside me all right, calmly and persuasively trying to separate me from God. In his seductive whisper, he listed the horrors being done to my family and friends as proof of God's absence and indifference. "Would the God you've prayed to since childhood let babies be raped, then roasted alive . . . would he leave you here, alone with me and my killers? You know that the answer is no, Immaculée. You know your God is letting your mother and father be murdered at this very moment. Your God is just a lie. Listen carefully to me now, I am telling the truth. The killers are coming for you—they are in the next room. Call out to them, and your pain will end."

At that moment, for the first of many times to follow in the coming months, I heard the killers in the house. They moved from room to room, opening cupboard doors and emptying drawers as they tore through every possible hiding place. Soon, I heard them standing outside the pastor's bedroom, just a few feet away and in full view of the flimsy bathroom door that concealed us. A mantra of doom ran through my mind in a terrifying loop: *They see the door; they've found you. They see the door; they've found you. They see the door; they've found you.* The devil's voice boomed in my head like an enormous, deafening bell.

I clutched my father's red-and-white rosary and prepared to pray as I have never prayed before.

I called on God, but my faith was flagging and the beads felt as heavy as boulders in my hand. Satan's voice was so convincing, my prayers so stifled, and my terror so great, that nothing would have been easier than yielding to that demonic advice and crying out to the killers to open the door and slaughter us one by one.

But I became aware of another presence as well, like a gentle hand held just above my head waiting to comfortingly stroke my brow the moment I turned my face toward heaven.

THE FAITH I HAD NURTURED, and that had been nurtured in me all of my life, had maintained a thread of truth between God and me. I remember hearing somewhere that praying the rosary was like pulling on a rope that bent heaven toward Earth, and I never needed to feel God's heavenly presence near me as much as I did at that very moment.

I tried so hard to pray the rosary but my lips and mind were paralyzed with fear, my skin was on fire, and I was certain I was about to die. My eyes widened painfully and my vision telescoped toward the handle of the door. I was certain I saw it beginning to turn. I pushed my rosary in my mouth in a last attempt to free my prayers and begged God with all my heart to please keep the killers away from me.

I must have passed out from terror because the next thing I was aware of was Pastor Murinzi standing in the doorway several hours later recounting how the killers had ransacked the entire house searching for us. "They got a tip I was hiding Tutsi women. They even came into my bedroom, and one of them was about to open the bathroom door. Lucky for all of us, he turned around just then and said he had to go home. But he promised he would be more thorough when they came back to search again."

My heart sickened when I realized that the killers would be back again and again. Would we live through this nightmare for days or weeks or even months without end? I looked at my companions and saw that they were trembling even harder than I was. There was no way my heart or mind could endure this amount of stress and panic.

Crouched on my knees, I clasped my hands together and held my rosary toward God. I thanked Him for sparing us from the killer at the door, but then begged Him to either take us immediately or show me how to blind the killers every time they approached the bathroom. And just like that, He responded.

No sooner had I said "Amen" than an image of a large wardrobe in the pastor's bedroom flashed through my mind—to be precise, it was an image of the wardrobe standing in front of the bathroom door, blocking it completely from sight. I didn't remember seeing the wardrobe before, especially since we had been hustled through the pastor's house and into the bathroom during the dead of night and practically in pitch dark. Yet there it was in my head, suddenly emblazoned upon my thoughts as surely as if God had burned it into my brain with a branding iron.

I looked up at the pastor and told him what he had to do: he had to push the wardrobe in front of the bathroom door immediately or else we would all surely be found and murdered. He resisted at first, illogically fearing greater reprisals from the killers if they thought he went to extra lengths to hide us. But I spoke to him with the conviction that can come only from one who truly believes God has spoken to them.

I begged the pastor to yield to me, and he did. He moved the wardrobe in front of the door, and that simple act saved our lives on more than one occasion.

# CHAPTER 9

# OPENING PRAYERS

My head and my heart still writhed in fear, anger, and confusion, the likes of which I'd never known before. The devil's voice that had twisted through my mind as the killers searched the house had been silenced when I called on God to save us, but the terror was already returning, my mouth filled with nervous bile and my entire body quaked.

And sure enough, as soon as the sun set and I heard the sounds of screaming in the distant darkness, the devil began whispering to me once again. I knew that only God could silence that slithering voice, so I vowed to pray throughout the night without rest.

I began the first of the rosary's opening prayers by squeezing the crucifix of my father's beads between my thumb and forefinger with such force that the metal grew hot against my skin. I made the Sign of the Cross and silently said the rosary's first prayer. Perhaps for the first time in the thousands of times I'd said it, I fully understood and completely meant every word.

"In the name of the Father, and of the Son, and of the Holy Spirit. Amen."

The devil's voice was suddenly banished by this short, perfect prayer. The words were my declaration that I was about to do something with the backing of the most powerful force in the universe: the Father of all Creation; His son, the embodiment of all good; the Holy Spirit, the power of God's love within us.

It dawned on me that as a child of God, part of that power belonged to me. I realized my words meant: "By the power invested in me by God Himself, I begin this prayer!" It was the most positive and empowering phrase ever to pass my lips, yet my heart had never been more humble. I spent at least two hours contemplating this one prayer, and was only pulled out of my reflection by the cries of someone being attacked a few hundred yards from the house.

I shivered, said a prayer that the soul of the poor person whose life had just ended be guided quickly to heaven, then plunged back into my rosary . . . silently commencing the second prayer that is said while holding the crucifix: the Apostles' Creed. This prayer had always been a chore for me, repeating that I believed in God, then what the Bible says about Jesus and the Holy Spirit and the Church and Saints and on and on and on, was just so . . . *redundant*. It seemed a pointless prayer because if I didn't believe all those things in the first place, I wouldn't be praying the rosary!

However, the Creed took on new meaning for me while kneeling on the bathroom floor surrounded by killers. I realized that the words embodied the ethos of Christianity since Jesus first sent his apostles into the world to spread the Word of God. Just one day earlier, this prayer had meant so little to me. Now it was my spiritual compass. In a moment of clarity I recognized in its words who I was and where I stood in my faith. It gave me my bearings as a Christian, and provided me with the voice I needed to stand up and declare whose side I was on and what I believed in. I was a child of God and followed in the footsteps of Jesus, and no power on Earth—not the killer at the door or the devil in my ear—could ever take that away from me.

The fingers of my right hand moved from the crucifix to the first large bead of my rosary, and the words of the Lord's Prayer began tumbling from my heart. I felt God in the bathroom with me, as though He had answered me when I prayed "Our Father." I thought of Dad, leading thousands in the same prayer, holding this same rosary in his hand, and asking God for the same things I was asking Him for now: to deliver me from evil.

There was so much anger in my heart toward the killers at that moment that I could not bring myself to ask God to forgive their trespasses—their trespasses were too great, too vile . . . and they were still trespassing against me, against so many innocent people! I hated the killers and prayed for God to be patient with me.

My fingers moved toward the rosary's main chaplet, and I paused on each bead to delve into the meaning of the corresponding prayers with a passion and yearning unknown to me until that point. On each of the next three beads I prayed the Hail Mary, recalling my love of Our Lady over the years, and how she wept when she warned us of the coming genocide. Each of the three times I called her name I felt Our Mother's gentle, comforting hand on my shoulder—her touch would soon become my greatest solace.

On the next large bead I prayed the Glory Be prayer, wishing with all my being that God's glory would indeed, now and forever, be the driving force of all existence— a force against which the kind of evil now strangling Rwanda would stand no chance.

Then, on the same large bead, I said the rosary's final opening prayer before I would announce which mystery

I was about to meditate on. Again, the Fátima Prayer had never really made an impact on me before, simply because no one I had ever loved dearly had died, and the concept of my own death had never entered my youthful mind. All that had changed in a matter of a few days.

Death was now all around me—I didn't know if my parents or brothers were alive or even if I myself would survive the night. I had lost count of the number of screams I had heard coming from outside that had ended in wheezing death rattles. I pressed my beads to my lips and whispered: *O my Jesus, forgive us our sins, save us from the fires of hell, and lead all souls to heaven, especially those who are most in need of your mercy.*

As I was about to internally announce my intention to mediate upon the First Joyful Mystery, more screaming fell upon my ears from out of the darkness. Such little moonlight penetrated the bathroom through the room's one tiny window that I couldn't see the rosary in my hand, so I summoned an image of the red-and-white beads to my mind. Suddenly my thoughts were flooded with memories of the rosary throughout my life.

I saw myself as a young girl at home, kneeling and laughing with my brothers as our parents tried to ignore their noisome kids and meditate on a rosary mystery. A moment later I was on a mountaintop, kneeling with two of my little friends praying for the Virgin Mary to appear so I could be one of her visionaries, like the Fátima children, or Bernadette of Lourdes.

Then I saw Father Rwagema with his armful of rosaries heading off to Kibeho as I added mine to his pile. And there was Father Clement three different times: first in my backyard instructing me to always pray with my heart; then smiling at me after my rosary test when he told me I had a "perfect score"; and then after my confirmation, telling me to use the rosary to call on Mary in my hour of need.

There was Damascene's smile, brilliant and fine, as he instructed me on how to study using the rosary and praying the ideal number of Hail Marys . . . and there too was the sweet face of Pierre as the bus carried him away from me forever, just after the rosary had given us one perfect moment that would last a lifetime.

I saw my father sliding a new rosary toward me as he dropped me off at the Seventh-day Adventist school, telling me to hold on to my faith and use the rosary to ward off the demons of the world. Then I saw him again, as he was only a few days ago: first as he held his rosary high and called upon the multitude to repent their sins and to pray, and then as he handed me that same rosary—the rosary I now held in my hands—as he told me to call upon Mary when I no longer had him in my life.

When I heard Pastor Murinzi's roosters crowing, I realized that I had been reflecting on my own life with the rosary instead of the mystery I had intended to start. But through that personal reflection I was able to see how the rosary had always been with me, and how on so many occasions I'd used it to call for help when I needed it most. I also recalled how Father Clement reminded me of the importance of developing a deep understanding of the mysteries to truly appreciate the full meaning and power of the rosary. I resolved to do just that for however long I would be trapped in the bathroom.

So when the pastor checked on us that morning, I asked him to lend me a Bible. I then began to study the life of Jesus and Mary with a mind now focused entirely on learning all they had to teach. The Bible and my rosary were the only weapons I had to fight for my life.

I DIDN'T WAIT FOR THE KILLERS to arrive at the door to open my heart in prayer. After their first visit to the house I knew that fear and despair would be ever present in my life. When I wasn't praying or reading the word of God, I was in torment. The only thing that stilled my anguish and silenced the devil's voice was prayer.

I quickly learned that, with my rosary in hand and my heart humbled before God, I could open a door in my mind and step out of the bathroom to be with Him. By the time I finished the rosary's opening prayers I'd feel a warmth in the center of my chest, as though a glowing ember had been placed beside my heart; after making the Sign of the Cross, that warmth would radiate throughout my entire body. My state of mind became so peaceful that by the time I chose the mystery I intended to meditate on, the bathroom was a blur to me, the shouts of the killers—whether they were outside or searching within the house—were a barely noticed thrum of background noise.

If my heart was sincere, my fingers danced along the beads and my thoughts dropped like a stone in a deep pool of cool, clear, quenching water. My body was still on the hard tile floor, wedged beneath the other women crammed into the tiny space with me, but my mind was no longer in the pastor's house, no longer in Rwanda—it was with Jesus and Mary in the Holy Land.

I was not hallucinating or experiencing any kind of psychotic break; I was always conscious that, somewhere just behind me or in front of me, armed men were trying to murder me. But my rosary carried me to a place of such deep prayer that the mysteries I meditated on became as real to me as any waking experience or any memory I had of my own life. My prayerful state wasn't a daydream or surrender to a hyperactive imagination; rather, I was engaged in an active conversation with heaven.

When meditating upon a mystery I felt the same way I did when I was a child sitting beside a wood fire, with my head resting comfortably on my mother's lap. It wasn't my earthly mother's lap in which my head rested now, however, it was the lap of Mother Mary. If I opened my eyes while I was praying, I'd see the beautiful face of Our Lady smiling down at me, calming my soul with her loving presence. Sometimes it was as though she were showing me a movie. If I was confused or frightened, she calmed me wordlessly by softly touching my hair, stroking my cheek, or putting an image in my mind that resolved my question.

As you will soon see, it was through meditating on the mysteries of the rosary with the Blessed Mother at my side that I found the courage, strength, and faith that saved my life, and saved my soul.

Now, the idea that I was sitting and chatting with the Virgin Mary while praying the rosary may seem strange to some people, but it didn't to me. Not then and not now. What is sometimes hard for me to believe is how, sitting in the center of the most wretched killing fields the world has ever seen, I was repeatedly able to reach a near-blissful state of prayer. Yet that is exactly what happened to me. While enduring unbearable suffering, I received the most beautiful gift I've ever gotten: I discovered how to pray the rosary, find the Blessed Mother, and talk to the Lord. I discovered how to appreciate and receive the full beauty and power these precious beads offer to each and every one of us.

Reflecting on the Mysteries of the Holy Rosary deepened my understanding of God and my place in His kingdom more than anything else I've ever seen or done. The lessons I learned through meditating upon these mysteries delivered me from the evil of the genocide and showed me how to let go of the anger and hatred I felt toward the men who killed my family.

Learning the secrets of the rosary has been a long journey for me that, in many ways, I am still just beginning. I discover new meaning and more blessings in the mysteries every time I kneel to pray. I sincerely hope you will continue on this wonderful journey with me as we travel to the very heart of the rosary: the mysteries.

———•———

# PART II

# THE JOYFUL MYSTERIES

### (Traditionally Prayed on Mondays and Saturdays)

# CHAPTER 10

# THE FIRST JOYFUL MYSTERY

## The Annunciation

The first time I felt Mary sitting beside me cradling my head in her lap was during a predawn visit the killers paid on Pastor Murinzi. The exhausted pastor pleaded with the angry men to go away and come back at a civilized hour to conduct their killing. But they pushed their way inside, screaming for him to hand over "the female cockroaches" he was hiding.

In the bathroom, my own paralyzing fear was reflected back to me in the terrified eyes of the other women. I held up my rosary, made the Sign of the Cross, and began saying the opening prayers. The petrifying stomping and vicious shouts quickly faded away, and my pounding heart slowed to a calm, steady beat. And as soon as I whispered my intention to meditate on the First Joyful Mystery, I was no longer in the bathroom: I was with the Blessed Mother. My head resting peacefully in her lap, her hand stroking my hair, and my eyes widening in delight and wonder watching an amazing scene unfold before me.

There she was, a beautiful young woman—just a girl, really—alone in her room, a room that reminded me of my own childhood bedroom. The bedchamber slowly filled with a pool of warm, golden light; and a soft, musical voice lovingly greeted Mary by name. It was the Angel Gabriel, announcing that from among all the women on Earth, God had chosen Mary to be the Mother of the Lord and give birth to the baby Jesus.

I watched spellbound as the confused young woman replied that she was a virgin, so it was impossible for her to give birth. Gabriel explained that nothing was beyond God's power, and soon the Holy Spirit would come upon her and place the spirit of Jesus within her womb. I shook with nervous anticipation as the innocent maiden absorbed the full meaning of the angel's prophetic words.

When I was a young girl in Bible class, a nun told me that at this very moment—just after Gabriel delivered God's message to Mary—everything in heaven came to a standstill, and the entire heavenly host waited breathlessly for the virgin girl's answer. When she finally answered yes by saying, "Behold, I am the handmaiden of the Lord," all of heaven erupted in a celebration so joyous that the cheers and trumpet blasts echoed across the universe and will continue to reverberate throughout eternity.

As I listened to Mary say yes to Gabriel, goose bumps of delight rose on my skin. I cuddled more deeply into the Holy Mother's lap and she squeezed my hand ever so gently, signaling that she was pleased by the joy I took in her answer to Gabriel so long ago. One day that answer would cause her unimaginable pain, but that didn't seem to matter to her . . . I suppose she accepted her sacrifice because of her loving, immaculate heart. She knew that through personal pain she would help bring love, hope, and salvation to the rest of humankind.

IF YOU HAVE NEVER READ this beautiful story, you'll find it in your Bible in the Gospel of Luke. (As I will with each of the mysteries I am about to share with you, I'm including the biblical account here so you can reflect upon it in your own fashion and in your own time.)

In the sixth month the angel Gabriel was sent by God to a town in Galilee called Nazareth, to a virgin engaged to a man whose name was Joseph, of the house of David. The virgin's name was Mary. And he came to her and said, "Greetings, favored one! The Lord is with you." But she was much perplexed by his words and pondered what sort of greeting this might be. The angel said to her, "Do not be afraid, Mary, for you have found favor with God. And now, you will conceive in your womb and bear a son, and you will name him Jesus. He will be great, and will be called the Son of the Most High, and the Lord God will give to him the throne of his ancestor David. He will reign over the house of Jacob forever, and of his kingdom there will be no end."

Mary said to the angel, "How can this be, since I am a virgin?" The angel said to her, "The Holy Spirit will come upon you, and the power of the Most High will overshadow you; therefore the child to be born will be holy; he will be called Son of God. And now, your relative Elizabeth in her old age has also conceived a son; and this is the sixth month for her who was said to be barren. For nothing will be impossible with God." Then Mary said, "Here am I, the servant of the Lord; let it be with me according to your word." Then the angel departed from her (Luke 1:26–38).

As I thought about the story of the Annunciation I couldn't help but draw parallels between Mary's life and my own. This happens every time I meditate on the mysteries and it helps me immensely by bringing me closer to the humanity of the Holy Family, and by helping me see how they overcame or endured all the very human problems and challenges they faced. I am filled with admiration (and always learn a great deal) as I read about how they coped with hazards, heartaches, great loss, and unimaginable suffering, armed with only the simple tools of faith and unconditional love. During each meditation I have always tried to feel what Mary felt when forced to make such monumental choices and decisions.

When reflecting on this story while in hiding, I faced death daily and was in horrible physical and mental anguish. There was nothing I wanted more than to end my pain, and that solution could have been so simple for me—all I had to do was shout out to the killers. It is what the devil wanted me to do, and he presented me with a choice: constant suffering or instant release from my pain. He egged me on and pushed me to make the easy decision, to turn my back on God and take the quick way out with a single suicidal action.

Then I pondered Mary kneeling before Gabriel. She too was asked by a supernatural being to make an agonizingly difficult decision. Yet the angel's request of her was to bear the child of God—what an incomprehensible responsibility in itself! Beyond the concern of accepting that superhuman undertaking, this young virgin was being asked to conceive a child out of wedlock. For an unwed woman, pregnancy in those days meant becoming a social pariah, shunned by all but those who loved her most.

As a girl who grew up in a similarly conservative society, I completely related to Mary's dilemma! I saw what happened when one of my schoolmates became pregnant—she was banned from school and even her own family rejected her. I tried to help her, but her shame was so great she left our village never to be heard from again. Only God knows what happened to her and her poor child in a country so harshly judgmental and unforgiving for even the slightest lapse of female modesty.

When Mary was asked to accept the task of carrying the Son of God and raising him in a world that would reject and crucify him, this innocent child did not hesitate to do what her heart told her was right. She didn't ask Gabriel if her reputation would be protected; or if her fiancé, Joseph, would turn his back on her; or even if she would be stoned to death in the public square. She knew what was being asked of her and accepted the suffering it would bring in her wonderfully humble way: "Here am I, the servant of the Lord."

God did not force Mary to say yes; instead, Gabriel presented her with a choice. She chose to do the right thing, even though it was the most difficult choice to make. She said yes despite her fear and her belief that what she was being asked to do was beyond her grasp and capabilities. Her deep faith and love of God allowed her to trust Him with her life—she was His obedient servant, and her happy duty was to let His will be done.

As the Blessed Mother comforted me while we shared this miraculous moment in her life, I was struck by the awesome power of God to work miracles in *all* our lives. Although Mary didn't hesitate to say yes to God, she knew that giving birth was impossible for a virgin. In wonderful simplicity Gabriel revealed the power of God, saying essentially that He would work a miracle in Mary's life. Then Gabriel immediately announced the second miracle found in this story: that Mary's childless cousin Elizabeth, barren and long past her childbearing years, was pregnant with Jesus's cousin, John the Baptist.

As Gabriel reminded Mary, no matter how weak and helpless we mortals are, nothing is impossible for God. So I had to trust that, no matter how hopeless I felt in the pastor's bathroom surrounded by killers, I would emerge alive and well, even if that required a miracle.

RESTING MY HEAD IN MARY'S LAP as I meditated made it easy for me to forget the horror around me, both in the bathroom and in the future . . . that is, if I survived and stepped out into the aftermath of the genocide. Through Mary's example I realized that no matter how difficult life might become, how rejected and reviled I may be by society, and how inviting taking the easy way out could be, my love of God demanded I do the right thing. I would do my best to ignore the devil's voice, remain a servant of God, and put myself in His loving hands, as Mary had, and trust in Him to guide me home.

As I sensed I was drawing to an end of my reflection on the First Joyful Mystery, I folded my hands together and sent this prayer to my Father in heaven:

*Dear God, I know You must be listening to me. You have shown that you are up there, and I know for sure now and beyond all doubt that You exist. You understand what I am going through and the fear that is torturing my heart. I am begging You to save us . . . I know that You love me so much that You sent Your son to save me through Mary . . . a woman just like me, an innocent girl, a human being. You must love* us deeply to send us Your only son to die so horribly for our sins to be cleansed.

I know now how merciful You are, so my sins can't be an obstacle between us . . . especially because I am asking for pardon in every way possible for anything I have done that has been against Your loving way. But I understand You are busy . . . I know there are many people dying, many innocent people that need Your help. Maybe I shouldn't be praying to be saved . . . maybe I am being selfish, but You have said to ask for what we want, and I want to live! I believe in You, and if I'm smart I will believe every word You say.

You say we should forgive, but sometimes I pray for the killers to die . . . please forgive me . . . but I don't want them to find me and kill me and kill other innocent people . . . it's so complicated, my dear God . . . how can You love them and love me? I know I can't lie to You, so You know I hate them and want them dead! I will try not to wish for that again. I will try to be strong and follow Your commandments . . . You have shown me the strength of the girl You chose to carry your son and bring him into this world.

I ask you to give me some of the strength of my Blessed Mother. You see, I know how weak I am. If I trusted in You fully I would not be this terrified . . . I would not be so frightened that I want to let someone kill me to end my pain. Please be with me as you were with Mary and Joseph when they faced persecution and ridicule. They were mocked and abused, they suffered, but You gave them the strength to carry on. I suppose I have to accept my pain because it is said that anything good in life is born with pain, like having children. Because all that matters is trusting in You. I will walk through this terrible pain as far as I *can as long as You will lead me, and I can hold the hand of the Blessed Mother in prayer.*

*But God, in the Bible You tell us that if we ask we shall receive. I am asking You, please, please, please don't let the killers find us. No matter what pain I might be going through now, I truly do want to live and serve You, and I don't want to die in such terrible fear. Please take care of my parents and my brothers, and please promise to hear their prayers as well. Thank You. Amen.*

—•—

# CHAPTER 11

# THE SECOND
# JOYFUL MYSTERY

## The Visitation

As soon as I announced my intention to pray the Second Joyful Mystery, I found my head once again in the Blessed Mother's lap, and the two of us watched together as she made the journey to visit her cousin Elizabeth.

It began as the First Joyful Mystery had, with the radiant young Mary on her own. This time she was not in her room, though, but traveling along a hilltop that overlooked much of the Holy Land. Her head and hair were modestly concealed beneath a scarf as she walked hurriedly along a county road flanked by rows of olive trees. The rolling hills of the countryside reminded me of the hilly landscape of Rwanda, and I worried for Mary's safety because she was alone. Yet I knew that Mary's heart compelled her to make this visit to her cousin, and that she was being watched over from above. Soon my concerns evaporated and it seemed I was walking along with her—I felt the coolness of a high-country breeze against my skin and the need to shield my eyes against the midday sun.

Mary stopped in front of a small thatched-roof house. She pulled the scarf from her head, revealing her beautiful, glowing face, which reflected the health of the baby Jesus, whom she carried in her womb. She stepped through the doorway and was immediately welcomed by Elizabeth, her much older cousin, whose face beamed with love. Mary's affection for her cousin reverberated in her simple greeting: "Cousin!"

Elizabeth clasped her rounded belly, in which she nurtured the unborn John the Baptist. She smiled as her baby sensed the presence of Jesus nearby and leapt for joy in her womb. The two female cousins could be mistaken for mother and daughter and loved each other like sisters, yet they were no longer tied only by bonds of blood. They were now linked by divine intervention, through the love and the will of God. My eyes filled with the same tears of happy wonderment streaming down the women's cheeks as they rejoiced in knowing that they were both serving God. I was swept up in the joy passing between the two soon-to-be mothers.

Elizabeth, filled with the Holy Spirit, threw her arms as wide apart as she possibly could, sank to her knees, and shouted a welcome to Mary that has echoed through the ages—a welcome repeated a billion times around the world each day by those inviting Mary and Jesus into their hearts while praying the rosary: "Blessed art thou among women, and blessed is the fruit of thy womb!"

Mary's response to Elizabeth, also alive with the love of the Holy Spirit, sent shivers along my spine. In a cadence as sweet and as softly powerful as the most delicate flute, the young girl raised her voice in song: "My soul magnifies the Lord, and my spirit rejoices in God my Savior, for he has looked with favor on the lowliness of his servant."

MARY'S WORDS HAVE ALSO BEEN immortalized in my all-time favorite hymn, the Magnificat, which appears in prose form below. There was no need for me to hear the rest of the words they exchanged, for I had already committed them to memory long ago:

---

In those days Mary set out and went with haste to a Judean town in the hill country, where she entered the house of Zechariah and greeted Elizabeth. When Elizabeth heard Mary's greeting, the child leaped in her womb. And Elizabeth was filled with the Holy Spirit and exclaimed with a loud cry, "Blessed art thou among women, and blessed is the fruit of thy womb. And why has this happened to me, that the mother of my Lord comes to me? For as soon as I heard the sound of your greeting, the child in my womb leaped for joy. And blessed is she who believed that there would be a fulfillment of what was spoken to her by the Lord."

And Mary said, "My soul magnifies the Lord, and my spirit rejoices in God my Savior, for he has looked with favor on the lowliness of his servant. Surely, from now on all generations will call me blessed; for the Mighty One has done great things for me, and holy is his name. His mercy is for those who fear him from generation to generation. He has shown strength with his arm; he has scattered the proud in the thoughts of their hearts. He has brought down the powerful from their thrones, and lifted up the lowly; he has filled the hungry with good things, and sent the rich away empty. He has helped his servant Israel, in remembrance of his mercy, according to the promise he made to our ancestors, to Abraham and to his descendants forever."

> And Mary remained with her about three months
> and then returned to her home (Luke 1:39–56).

Reflecting upon this beautiful passage today touches and inspires me in completely different ways than it did while I was in hiding—even now, as I write down the words from Luke, I receive lessons in how to better live my life and better serve God and my fellow human beings.

One of the enduring beauties of the rosary is its power to draw our attention to the aspects of our life most in need of help, comfort, or guidance. So every time we meditate on a mystery, or read the corresponding Bible passage, certain words or ideas will sing out to us—perhaps because they spark a happy family memory or shed light on how to resolve a persistent challenge. The point is that when we pray the rosary, sweetness slips into our bloodstream and slowly works its way through our entire body. Many times when I pray it I don't realize until much later that my problems have been solved, and only then by noticing my spirit has lightened, a smile has crept onto my face, and what had seemed an insurmountable difficulty no longer concerns me at all.

The problems that plagued me constantly during the genocide were not so easy to forget. I was in constant peril of losing my faith, my life, and my salvation.

When I reflected on the Visitation while in hiding, I was first struck by Mary's love for Elizabeth and her willingness to travel to help her cousin, who had entered the third trimester of her pregnancy with John the Baptist. At that point Mary was carrying Jesus in her own womb; traveling any distance beyond her own village was risky. There were countless dangers on the road, such as bandits, snakebites or animal attack, or a dozen other potential calamities.

Yet because Mary knew that her cousin was in need, she did not hesitate to go to her aid. She acted as Jesus wants us all to act, by loving our neighbor as we love ourselves. It was an act of charity that we could all take a lesson from.

I was also moved and enlightened to see how the middle-aged Elizabeth humbled herself by kneeling down to the teenaged Mary. I have remarked before that there are striking similarities between the culture of ancient Israel and the Rwanda in which I grew up. When I was a girl it was unheard of for an older person to show any deference to someone younger, never mind kneeling down to them! The same was true, I have been told, in the society in which Mary and Elizabeth were raised. That is what makes Elizabeth's gesture of supplication so remarkable—to me it meant that God had blessed her with the clarity of mind to realize that, although the girl standing in front of her was just her little cousin, in truth, she was addressing the mother of Our Savior.

As far as I can see, Elizabeth is the first person in the Bible to treat Mary with a reverence due to the woman who was chosen to bring the Lord into the world. As Mary said (with humility) to her cousin, "Surely, from now on all generations will call me blessed; for the Mighty One has done great things for me, and holy is his name."

It also struck me that Elizabeth had been able to look beyond the physical appearance of her cousin and fully appreciate the divine spark shining within her the same divine spark God has placed in the soul of all of His children. Upon her arrival at Elizabeth's house after an arduous journey, the weary and dust-covered Mary must have, despite her radiant beauty, looked like a dirty and disheveled child. Yet Elizabeth greeted her as though she

was a queen—and, as it turned out, Mary would indeed be hailed one day as the Queen of Heaven and Earth.

WHILE REFLECTING ON THIS I was reminded of a miracle Father Clement had told me about when I was quite young. It involved a Polish nun named Sister Faustina, who many people were saying should be made a saint. (In fact, the Vatican declared Sister Faustina to be a saint in 2000, the first one of the 21st century! She is now best known for her diaries and mystical visions, particularly her vision of Jesus's Divine Mercy, which has been expressed in several famous and iconic paintings.)

When Father Clement told me about her, all he said was that she was born in Poland in 1905, grew up in terrible poverty, and found joy in serving God and helping the poor. One day Jesus appeared to her disguised as a beggar, and Sister Faustina doted on him with the same kindness and generosity she offered everyone she met. Jesus revealed to her who he really was and said the message of his visit was this: *We all carry God within us, and God comes to us in many forms. By treating everyone as a child of God, we will never miss an opportunity to serve Him.*

I remember thinking how wonderful it would be if we all followed that simple rule. If people welcomed others into their lives as Elizabeth had welcomed Mary, or as Sister Faustina welcomed the beggar who was Jesus, there would be no war or genocide in the world. Hatred, abuse, and suffering would be miraculously replaced with love, kindness, and tolerance.

At that time my own neighbors were coming to kill me, instead of coming to help me as Mary had come to help Elizabeth. My neighbors viewed me as a cockroach to be exterminated, not as a daughter of God to be cherished, or a cousin in Christ to be loved. Because their hearts

overflowed with hatred, they had completely lost sight of
God's love. I vowed that if I survived the genocide, I would
not let hatred turn my heart to stone or blind me to the
divine spark that dwells within us all.

However, I knew that if I ever hoped to see beyond
the blood on the killers' hands and be able to rejoice in
the God within them, I would first have to purge my own
heart of the anger and hatred I felt toward them. I also
knew I would never be capable of doing that on my own,
without the power of God's love. And so I prayed:

*Dear Father, thank You again for sending Your
son to us through the Blessed Virgin, and for the love
and tenderness Mary and Elizabeth shared. Their
visit has shown me how You want neighbors to love
and honor each other, and how You want us to love
and respect Our Lady. Please help my neighbors remember that they once loved me and my family, and
that they can love us again if they open their heart
to Your son. Fill their hearts with love, God, so they
will put down their machetes and stop hurting us and
hurting themselves.*

*Thank You for teaching me the importance of hu-
mility by showing me through this mystery how humble Mary and Elizabeth were when they encountered
Your greatness and glory. I want to have a humble
heart, Father, but it is hard for me.*

*In the Magnificat, Mary sang that with the
strength of Your arm You "brought down the powerful
from their thrones, and lifted up the lowly . . . filled
the hungry with good things, and sent the rich away
empty." Even though I know I should pray for the killers, I want You to bring them down from their thrones
and lift us lowly Tutsis up so we can have justice.*

*I know that is not humility, and the justice I want is really revenge, which is against Your commandant for us to love . . . forgive me for that.*

*Please give me the strength You gave Elizabeth and Sister Faustina to see beyond appearances . . . help me see and celebrate the goodness you placed in all Your children . . . even when those children do such horrible, ugly things. I also know that Jesus told Sister Faustina he has great mercy toward sinners, and I am a sinner, so I hope You have mercy upon me. And I am thinking that if You are able to make Elizabeth pregnant at that age, protecting me from the killers is not so hard for You.*

*I know many of the innocent souls being killed are much better people than I am. I don't know what You are discussing with them, or if You are giving them courage or the grace to accept death . . . but in my heart there is this need to live, so please don't let me die on this dirty floor!*

*Please hear my prayer, and please watch over my family because I don't know what has happened to them. Amen.*

# CHAPTER 12

# THE THIRD JOYFUL MYSTERY

## The Nativity

If anything could be described as a happy experience for me while I was in hiding, it would have to be witnessing the baby Jesus's arrival into this world while meditating on the Third Joyful Mystery.

At first, as I sat with Mary to watch the events unfold, I was nervous as could be for the expectant young mom and her fiancé, Joseph. But since I knew that things would work out, I was slowly able to relax and enjoy what I was seeing.

There in front of me was Joseph, a gentle-looking, dark-haired man with a beard, who wore a look of concern stamped upon his brow as he led a donkey that carried a very pregnant Mary. The authorities had ordered them to travel to Joseph's birthplace of Bethlehem to fill out census forms, and the trip had taken longer than expected. They were just getting into town as the sun was going down, and rushing to find a place to stay in case Mary went into labor. The poor woman looked so uncomfortable atop the bouncing beast, with her legs dangling in a sidesaddle fashion, as she clutched the donkey's mane with one hand and cradled her swollen belly with the other. Her beautiful face looking deeply troubled as she gauged how far they still were from town, with darkness closing in around them.

Although Bethlehem was Joseph's birthplace, he no longer had family there whom he could call on. When he and Mary finally entered the town, he realized he knew no one at all who could put them up. He frantically pulled the donkey carrying his beloved from one inn to the next, desperately seeking a bed in which she could give birth. But his appearance put people off, as he looked poor and ragged and as though he didn't have a penny in his pocket. He was turned away from every door he knocked upon. As night deepened, Mary cried out that her time had arrived. Joseph shouted through the dark streets begging for someone, anyone, to have mercy upon a pregnant woman and to take her in for just one night. No answer came.

I lifted my head from her lap and looked up at Mary for reassurance—and saw her smiling at me. In my mind I heard a gentle voice say that all was going according to God's plan. Suddenly I heard trumpets all around me and a choir that sounded like a hundred thousand sweet-voiced altar boys singing in unison, "Glory, glory, glory be to God in the highest!"

When I turned back to the streets of Bethlehem I saw Mary surrounded in a golden haze as she lay on a pile of hay in an open cowshed, much like the one my father had built behind our family's home to shelter cattle, the one my brothers had to shovel dung from each morning before school. Joseph was kneeling on Mary's left side, holding her hand; on her right, wrapped in fresh cloth and tucked comfortably into a straw-filled water trough doubling as a cradle, was the most beautiful baby anyone had ever laid eyes upon.

The newborn boy seemed to glow from within. He didn't cry, or even make a whimper. His angelic face was serene as his young eyes tried to focus on the three strangers who had unexpectedly arrived at the stable. The trio began excitedly relaying to the new parents how an angel had appeared to them while they were tending their sheep, and led them to this very spot to behold the savior of mankind.

Mary seemed more delighted than surprised by their news and smiled as the young shepherds walked away into the night singing God's praises at the top of their lungs.

I HAD JUST WITNESSED THE GREATEST childbirth story in human history, and I knew that whenever I wanted to relive the wonderful moment, all I had to do was open my Bible.

---

In those days a decree went out from Emperor Augustus that all the world should be registered. This was the first registration and was taken while Quirinius was governor of Syria. All went to their own towns to be registered. Joseph also went from the town of Nazareth in Galilee to Judea, to the city of David called Bethlehem, because he was descended from the house and family of David. He went to be registered with Mary, to whom he was engaged and who was expecting a child. While they were there, the time came for her to deliver her child. And she gave birth to her firstborn son and wrapped him in bands of cloth, and laid him in a manger, because there was no place for them in the inn.

In that region there were shepherds living in the fields, keeping watch over their flock by night. Then an angel of the Lord stood before them, and the glory of the Lord shone around them, and they were terrified. But the angel said to them, "Do not be afraid; for see—I am bringing you good news of great joy for all the people: to you is born this day in the city of David a Savior, who is the Messiah, the Lord. This will be a sign for you: you will find a child wrapped in bands of cloth and lying in a manger." And suddenly there was with the angel a multitude of the heavenly host, praising God and saying, "Glory to God in the highest heaven, and on earth peace among those whom he favors!"

When the angels had left them and gone into heaven, the shepherds said to one another, "Let us go now to Bethlehem and see this thing that has taken place, which the Lord has made known to us." So they went with haste and found Mary and Joseph, and the child lying in the manger. When they saw this, they made known what had been told them about this child; and all who heard it were amazed at what the shepherds told them. But Mary treasured all these words and pondered them in her heart. The shepherds returned, glorifying and praising God for all they had heard and seen, as it had been told them (Luke 2:1–20).

As I meditated on what I had just beheld, I was most amazed by the extremely humble beginnings in which Our Lord chose to arrive in his human form. Jesus could have come to Earth as anyone—a rich man, a king, or even as the son of Augustus Caesar, the most powerful man in the world.

Instead, Christ chose to be born in the most beggarly circumstances possible, on the floor of a stable that housed farm animals. What was Jesus telling us by being born into such extreme poverty, surrounded only by the love of his earthly parents and heir to nothing but the promise given to all those who are very poor: hard work, scarcity, sacrifice, and struggle?

I reflected on what kind of life *I* had been born into. It is true that I was born in one of the poorest countries in the world, but I wasn't aware of that fact and never felt poor. By the standards of rural Rwandan life, my family was well-to-do. Most villagers in our community lived in single-room homes with dirt floors. When it was cold, people often slept in the same bed and kept their cows and goats in the room with them. My parents were teachers, Dad built our house himself, I had my own bedroom, and we had electricity for a couple of hours each day. My father even owned a car.

People came to my parents for help, advice, and financial assistance, and they never left disappointed. A lot of people in the area even referred to Dad as *muzungu*, which means "white man"—which means "rich man." So, compared to many, many people in Rwanda, I had it made. Yet while I always loved God and the Virgin Mary, and always had what I considered a rich prayer life, I never understood what spiritual wealth was until everything I'd ever owned and everyone I'd ever loved had been ripped away from me overnight.

As I lay on the bathroom floor listening to the killers prowling outside, I realized that my parents and brothers and friends were all likely dead or dying, my house and all I had was burned to ashes, and the world I had grown up in was gone and never coming back. All I had left were the clothes on my back, the rosary in my hand, and the prayers in my heart—and somehow, despite my fear, hunger, and suffering, it seemed to be so much more than I'd ever had before.

My sudden, complete poverty had enriched my communication with God a thousandfold. I had not been transformed into a saint or even a better person. But realizing that I actually owned nothing in this life, including my life, had forced me to focus on what was truly important: my eternal soul. And that was a lesson worth more to me than rubies. Seeing the Queen of Heaven giving birth to the Son of God in a dirty animal pen without a penny to her name or a friend in the world taught me that the Kingdom of God belonged to the rich in spirit.

Dwelling on this put me in mind of Father Damien, a Belgian priest I read about in high school who traveled to Hawaii in the 1860s, then volunteered to serve some of the poorest and most rejected people on the planet: the residents of the leper colony on the island of Molokai. Father Damien didn't just offer lip service to these impoverished outcasts; he lived among them until he became one with them, eventually contracting and dying of leprosy himself. As he once wrote to his brother in Europe, "I make myself a leper with the lepers to gain all to Jesus Christ."

Damien absolutely followed in Christ's footsteps—he embraced poverty and sacrificed himself to aid, comfort, and minister to the lowliest of the low. I know that he prayed the rosary often, which comforted me while I was in hiding. (Father Damien's faith was so great that, after his death, several people with fatal illnesses were miraculously cured—miracles that the Vatican recognized before pronouncing him a saint in 2009!)

IN PASTOR MURINZI'S BATHROOM, every time I recalled a story I had heard or read about concerning a miracle that had occurred through prayer, my faith in the rosary and my love of God would soar, as it still does.

My reflection upon Jesus's birth ended with my realization that it was easy to endure poverty and focus on the afterlife while cowering from killers in a cramped bathroom. I had nothing to lose and could be sent to meet my maker at any moment. But could I maintain my respect for the virtue of poverty if I survived the genocide and built a new and prosperous life in a distant future in a faraway country? I hoped I would, so I prayed:

*Dear Jesus, I watched you with your mother after you were born in a cow stable. You are a king, but you chose to be born a pauper because you love the poor and weak among us more than anyone else. You told all of us so many times in the Bible that poverty is not a curse, but can be a blessing in which we can discover the true meaning of faith. Like when you said, "Blessed are you who are poor, for yours is the kingdom of God. Blessed are you who are hungry now, for you will be filled. Blessed are you who weep now, for you will laugh."*

*I know that you are talking about the hungry and poor in spirit . . . but I am hungry in both ways. I need to feed on your love every day because when I don't, my physical hunger feels like it will chew through my ribs! I think I'm starving, Lord, and I have no strength at all without you. Please, feed me . . . I pray that one day I will be able to eat my fill and laugh again, Lord, even if it is not until I meet you in heaven.*

*And Lord, if I do live and you bring me safely out of the bathroom to a new life, please help me live as Father Damien lived, without love for the trappings of the world. Please help me love only those things that are of true value, and please fill me with a desire to help the poorest of your children.*

*As you said in the Book of Matthew: "Come, you that are blessed by my Father, inherit the kingdom prepared for you from the foundation of the world; for I was hungry and you gave me food, I was thirsty and you gave me something to drink, I was a stranger and you welcomed me, I was naked and you gave me clothing, I was sick and you took care of me, I was in prison and you visited me."*

*Thank you for sparing me another day, and please protect my family, wherever they are, Lord. Amen.*

# CHAPTER 13

# THE FOURTH JOYFUL MYSTERY

## The Presentation

I announced the Fourth Joyful Mystery with mixed emotions because, although it opens with a celebration, the celebration is tinged with sorrow. But as always, once I was sitting with my head in the lap of the Blessed Mother, my heart was light as a feather.

Mary and Joseph, happy new parents, are approaching the towering temple in the heart of Jerusalem, to dutifully present the circumcised newborn Jesus to God in keeping with Jewish custom. As they ascended the temple steps together they appeared to me the picture-perfect family. There was Mary, a sweet-faced, radiant young mother with her dark hair demurely hidden beneath a flowing head covering. She lovingly carried the baby Jesus in her arms who, although covered with warm wraps, seemed to emanate a golden light from deep within his tiny body. A few steps in front of the mother and child walked the older Joseph, clearing a path on the crowded stairway for his family to pass through, all the while keeping a protective eye on his beloved Mary and adopted son.

From my readings of the sometimes confusing Bible passage that relates this story, I knew that Mary had to take part in a traditional purification ritual before coming to the temple. As I understood it, according to religious law, women of that time and culture were required to be purified after going through the messy business of childbirth. (We had a similar custom in Rwanda where a new mother did not emerge from her home until a week after her child was born.)

Since Jesus's birth had been miraculous and Mary had remained a virgin, I thought the law should not apply to her. But the Blessed Mother, who was at my side all the while as I was meditating on this mystery, silently let me know that religious obligations must not be ignored, no matter who someone is—even if she happens to be the Mother of God. I wanted to object and say to her she was so pure she needed no cleansing ritual, but Our Lady quieted me with a gentle touch.

I watched as Joseph entered the temple, then opened his cloak to reveal two cooing turtledoves he had bought as an offering to God for this happiest of occasions—for Jesus's circumcision, in accordance with Hebraic religious law, fulfilled the covenant between God and the Jewish people. I could see the pride in Joseph's and Mary's eyes as all who passed them in the temple were transfixed by the otherworldly beauty of the truly breathtaking child Mary cradled in her arms.

And then the most remarkable thing happened. An old man named Simeon approached the Holy Family and reached out for the baby, and Mary happily placed the child in his arms. She had no fear of his harming

Jesus because she sensed the presence of the Holy Spirit upon him.

Simeon's eyes glowed with joy as he held the infant toward heaven and blessed him, and blessed the name of God. He told Mary and Joseph that the Holy Spirit informed him that he would never die until he had beheld the savior of mankind with his own aged eyes. Now that he had seen the Christ child, he said he welcomed death, "for my eyes have seen your salvation, which you have prepared in the presence of all peoples."

But as he returned Jesus to Mary's arms and blessed the Holy Family, Simeon prophesized that Mary would suffer greatly because of her son, that her heart would feel the pain of a stabbing spear as surely as Jesus himself would one day be speared. The old man's words stung me like wasps because I knew they were true, and I ached at the pain Mary would endure. The Blessed Mother sensed my sudden sadness and once again calmed my mind with the soft touch of her hand against my cheek. A moment later another prophet—an ancient and devout woman named Anna—approached Mary and, upon seeing Baby Jesus, instantly praised God for sending His Redeemer into the world from heaven.

The last image I had of the Holy Family on that day was as they passed through a gate in Jerusalem's mighty wall and led their donkey on the road back to Nazareth, where they would present Jesus to Mary's family for the first time. There they waited patiently, keeping Christ's true identity a family secret until his ministry began.

THE INTRICACIES OF THE RITUALS and prophecies of this mystery forced me to come back to it again and again, until my Bible would often just fall open to it:

When the time came for their purification according to the law of Moses, they brought him up to Jerusalem to present him to the Lord (as it is written in the law of the Lord, "Every firstborn male shall be designated as holy to the Lord"), and they offered a sacrifice according to what is stated in the law of the Lord, "a pair of turtledoves or two young pigeons."

Now there was a man in Jerusalem whose name was Simeon; this man was righteous and devout, looking forward to the consolation of Israel, and the Holy Spirit rested on him. It had been revealed to him by the Holy Spirit that he would not see death before he had seen the Lord's Messiah. Guided by the Spirit, Simeon came into the temple; and when the parents brought in the child Jesus, to do for him what was customary under the law, Simeon took him in his arms and praised God, saying, "Master, now you are dismissing your servant in peace, according to your word; for my eyes have seen your salvation, which you have prepared in the presence of all peoples, a light for revelation to the Gentiles and for glory to your people Israel." And the child's father and mother were amazed at what was being said about him. Then Simeon blessed them and said to his mother Mary, "This child is destined for the falling and the rising of many in Israel, and to be a sign that will be opposed so that the inner thoughts of many will be revealed—and a sword will pierce your own soul, too."

There was also a prophet, Anna the daughter of Phanuel, of the tribe of Asher. She was of a great age, having lived with her husband seven years after her marriage, then as a widow to the age of eighty-four. She never left the temple but worshipped there with fasting and prayer night and day. At that moment she came, and began to praise God and to speak about the child to all who were looking for the redemption of Jerusalem.

When they had finished everything required by the law of the Lord, they returned to Galilee, to their own town of Nazareth. The child grew and became strong, filled with wisdom; and the favor of God was upon him (Luke 2:22–40).

---

The first thing I began reflecting upon in this passage was what the Blessed Mother had silently said to me during my meditation, when I questioned the need for her to undergo a purification ritual: *We must not neglect our religious duties no matter who we are, or how holy we may be or think ourselves to be.* The very fact that I was hiding in the bathroom to escape being raped and murdered by my neighbors was a perfect illustration of what Our Lady meant. If Rwandans had prayed the rosary every day, the genocide very likely would never have happened!

I wondered how many times the Virgin Mary had appeared to people throughout the world in the past eight centuries since first appearing to St. Dominic with the same message: "Pray the rosary every day to keep your heart near to God." It is exactly what she had said in Kibeho when begging us to pray the rosary every day with all our hearts to avoid the coming genocide. And yet so few of us did—even me, who was such a devotee of the rosary and truly loved the Virgin Mary, was often guilty of not praying the rosary every day.

It was easy for me to find excuses. When I attended the Seventh-day Adventist school, for example, I said I was afraid of getting caught with such a seemingly Catholic item and kept my beads in my pocket most of the time. Other times I was out having fun with friends and couldn't make the time; or, if I'm totally honest, I just got bored with saying it and would give myself a break.

Suddenly I was aware of how easy it was for a day or two of skipping prayers to lead to taking a pass on Sunday Mass or church service, going to bed without saying evening prayers, or eating a meal without first gracefully thanking God for the food He provided for us. Little slips in our duties—be they religious, academic, or work-related; in our relationships or personal conduct—might not seem like a big deal at the time, but I now understood how little slips can snowball into a single disastrous fall.

When I came home to spend Easter vacation with my family my world was as it had always been, but because so many Rwandans had slipped up by not praying and then by holding on to their hatred, our entire country collapsed into a hellish nightmare that claimed a million lives.

From that moment forward I promised myself, and God, that I would never treat my spiritual obligations with anything but the fullest respect they deserved. Through the mystery I had just meditated upon I saw afresh that God, Jesus, and the Holy Spirit are the most important sources of love in our lives. But we do not get that love through osmosis. We must foster and nourish the sacred in our lives, and sanctify our hearts by inviting God into them through regular prayer and worship.

If we vigilantly tend to our spiritual duties, we cannot help but spread the love we will receive through our efforts to everyone we encounter—our spouses, children, bosses, co-workers, employees, and even strangers on the street. How different my village and homeland would have been if we all had dutifully sought God's grace in our day-to-day routine. The Blessed Mother had offered us a miraculous way to avoid the genocide by simply praying the rosary every day, but we refused to accept that miracle because we didn't want to invest 20 minutes of our daily lives to make it come true.

MARY AND JOSEPH ACTED AS MODELS for all of us to emulate, as they followed the religious law that governed their culture. Even though they carried Christ the Lord with them into the temple, they did not consider themselves above the duties God asked of everyone.

And when Simeon revealed the heartache that lay in store for the entire family, they did not shrink from their duties or ask God to relieve them of their obligations. What they did instead was to finish performing the worship and rituals required of them, and then quietly make their way home as a family. Afterward, they simply carried on with their lives, raising Jesus in a loving environment in which they all faithfully served the Lord and patiently awaited God's will to be done. So I prayed:

> *Dearest Father, thank You for showing me how important it is the keep the bonds of Your love tightly wrapped around my heart by coming to You in prayer every day. I know that right now I am surrounded by killers and that it is probably a big part of the reason I am coming to You so often and asking for Your help . . . I don't want to be murdered, and only You can save me.*
>
> *I am sorry if I am being selfish, but honestly, I really do see now that I should have prayed more often for Your love and forgiveness. Maybe if I had done that—if we had all done that—we would not be in this horrible, horrible situation.*
>
> *Not praying enough for Your love to guide my heart was sinful of me; it hurt others, it hurt me, and, worst of all, it hurt You. I don't have a priest with me*

*here to confess my sins to, so I hope You will forgive me for my lapses in seeking You out every day. Please forgive me all of my sins . . . and give me strength to follow the example of Mary and Jesus, who had no sin upon them at all yet went to the temple to please You, to glorify Your name, and to offer You their love and obedience.*

*Thank You for giving us the Holy Family to model ourselves after, and please, please, help my own family here on Earth . . . they are lost in the darkness and need Your protection as much as I do. Thank You, Father. Amen.*

# CHAPTER 14

# THE FIFTH
# JOYFUL MYSTERY

## The Finding of Jesus
## in the Temple

During the genocide one of the most emotionally charged mysteries for me to reflect upon was the Finding of Jesus in the temple. This mystery is a happy one about a family reunion—but, at least for me, the happiness is laced with heartbreak in an all-too-human way.

As always, once I'd said my introductory prayers and announced that I was going to reflect upon this mystery, I found myself at the Blessed Mother's side and was instantly presented with a wildly chaotic scene that materialized in front of us like a shimmering mirage. My senses were flooded with the scents, sounds, and dazzling colors dancing before me in the bustling avenues of ancient Jerusalem during Passover festivities nearly 2,000 years ago. The scene did not seem like a vision: I could smell dank straw strewn across the road, feel that I could pluck a fresh fig from the wooden stall of a nearby vendor, or even slap the backside of one of the many donkeys tethered to the stone water troughs running the length of a city block.

Above the din of the merchants and the thousands of people pushing through the streets in every direction, I could hear the mingling of male voices singing prayers. I lifted my head from Mary's lap to see where the harmonious chanting was coming from and marveled at the magnificent temple rising high above the streets as though it were a crown God had placed atop the city of David. It was my first glimpse at the structure from afar, and it was the most incredible building I had ever seen. I gazed at it awestruck until the Blessed Mother silently focused my attention on what most mattered in the tableaux she was presenting to me.

That's when I saw them, in the midst of a long mule caravan snaking its way through the hectic streets toward the city's main gate. It was Mary whom I noticed first, more than a decade older than when I last saw her in the temple. Despite the harsh conditions of living in a primitive world, she had matured into womanhood with grace, her flawless face and sparkling dark eyes even more deeply beautiful than in her radiant youth. Beside her was Joseph, looking strong, dark, and weathered from years of working outside. Both of them seemed preoccupied.

Several yards behind the Holy Couple, perched atop a donkey, sat a 12-year-old boy I could not have mistaken for anyone but Jesus. He was a strikingly handsome lad with delicate facial features, the same soft brown eyes of his mother, and a mop of dark curly hair. He radiated the familiar aura of golden light I'd seem emanating from the baby Jesus, and when he smiled it seemed the sun shone brighter upon them all—the way my brother Damascene's smile could instantly light up a room or lighten my sad moods.

The family had journeyed for several days in the caravan with friends and extended family, enduring the 70 long, hard miles from Nazareth to Jerusalem to be in the holy city to observe Passover. Now, with their mules laden with supplies and gifts for loved ones back home, they set off on the arduous return trip. They were busy saying good-bye to relatives who came to wish them off, and making last-minute checks of their belongings and mules.

Jesus was a well-liked boy and freely moved among his friends and family in the large group of travelers, sometimes spending hours or an entire day riding with his many uncles, aunts, and cousins. So no one noticed when he hopped off his donkey and turned to look back at the temple towering above the city. A moment later the boy stepped away from the caravan, disappearing in the swirling river of people that surged through the streets.

Everything faded to black. I stared into darkness for several seconds until an amber glow appeared in the distance, and I was able to make out the shape of dozens of tents scattered across a large campsite. The light grew brighter, a rooster crowed, donkeys brayed, and pots and pans clattered as dawn broke and the camp stirred to life.

Suddenly the early-morning stillness was shattered by a single agonizing scream that nearly cleaved my heart in two. The scream had arisen from the depths of the Blessed Mother's heart when she realized in horror that her beloved boy was missing. Everyone had assumed that Jesus was staying with someone else in the caravan, but after tearing the camp apart, Mary and Joseph faced the harrowing reality that has crushed so many parents' hearts since the beginning of time: their child had been lost or taken.

With my head still in her lap, I could feel the Blessed Mother reliving the pain of the awful episode even though a thousand generations had passed, and even though she and Jesus now dwelled together in Paradise. I wanted to reach out to console her—but it was she, as always, who comforted me, placing her loving hand on my head and directing me to focus on my meditation, no matter how painful.

I watched as Mary and Joseph searched and re-searched the campsite, even after the others in the caravan had packed and continued on their way toward Nazareth. The tortured looks of fear, anxiety, and self-recrimination etched across the faces of the frantic parents made my heart ache. I traveled along with them for two excruciating days and sleepless nights as they meticulously retraced their steps back to Jerusalem, searching the countless ravines they walked by, knocking on each door they passed, and stopping every stranger on the road to ask if they had seen a gentle-looking 12-year-old Nazarene boy who was on his own. But each inquiry was met with the devastating response: no.

Finally, on the third day, after Mary and Joseph had searched every street and alleyway in Jerusalem, I watched them enter the temple where, despite their shame at losing the Son of God, they had come to beg the Father for forgiveness and plead for Him to return their beloved child to them.

Their prayers were answered: there, standing in the middle of a large group of rabbis and religious scholars stood their preteen son discussing theology and answering the scholars' questions on the meaning and interpretation of scriptural readings.

Both parents were momentarily stunned by how learned the boy was, and by the deference and respect offered to him by the elders he was addressing. Mary was nearly swooning from hunger, lack of sleep, and the stress of the three-day search. But her love and anger carried her straight to Jesus, whom she immediately began scolding. How could he, she demanded to know, treat his parents so thoughtlessly? She was sick with worry, and poor Joseph was a nervous wreck!

Jesus calmly looked at his fuming mother and, with just a trace of confusion, asked her, "Why were you searching for me? Did you not know that I must be in my Father's house?"

Mary wanted to box the boy's ears, but instead wrapped her arms around him and hugged him to her breast with all the strength in her body; then she kissed him over and over again. She didn't let go of her son's hand, or stop kissing him, until they were many miles away from Jerusalem and well on their way back home, where Jesus would grow into his role of Messiah. And from that day forward, he always obeyed and honored his parents in accordance to God's commandment.

SOMETIMES I FIND THAT meditating on this mystery too intensely leaves me exhausted, so I am happy to have the option of reading it in the Bible:

---

Now every year his parents went to Jerusalem for the festival of the Passover. And when he was twelve years old, they went up as usual for the festival. When the festival was ended and they started to return, the boy Jesus stayed behind in Jerusalem, but his parents did not know it. Assuming that he was in the group of travelers, they went a day's journey. Then they started to look for him among their relatives and friends. When they did not find him, they returned to Jerusalem to search for him. After three days they found him in the temple, sitting among the teachers, listening to them and asking them questions. And all who heard him were amazed at his understanding and his answers. When his parents saw him they were astonished; and his mother said to him, "Child, why have you treated us like this? Look, your father and I have been searching for you in great anxiety." He said to them, "Why were you searching for me? Did you not know that I must be in my Father's house?" But they did not understand what he said to them. Then he went down with them and came to Nazareth, and was obedient to them. His mother treasured all these things in her heart. And Jesus increased in wisdom and in years, and in divine and human favor (Luke 2:41-52).

---

As I have indicated already, reflecting on this mystery was a deeply emotional endeavor for me during the months I was in hiding. Mary and Joseph suffering and worrying about Jesus's safety, combined with the guilt of losing him, were very familiar feelings just then. At the time I had no idea if my parents were alive or dead, or what had become of my brothers Damascene and Vianney. They had been with me one moment, and then they were gone.

Only God knew where they were and what was happening to them—when I started thinking about it, I became sick to my stomach. The horrible possibilities haunted my mind: *What is happening to my mother at this very moment? God forbid she is in the hands of the same vicious men hunting me. Where is my brave father? Has he been wounded while defending our neighbors from the killers and is now lying in a ditch calling out to me for help? And what of my darling brother Damascene, who would fight to the death to protect a perfect stranger from being harmed by the killers? And worst of all, what has become of Vianney, whom I allowed to leave the safety of the pastor's house? Would whatever harm that befell that innocent boy be forever on my conscience? And if my parents are alive, what horrible pain must they be enduring not knowing what was happening with me!*

The weight of these sorrows just about crushed me during my first weeks in hiding. Thank goodness I had yet to become a parent—I'm sure if I'd added maternal worry to that emotional chaos I would have been crippled completely. (I know that, many years later, even losing sight of my daughter in a New York supermarket for a few minutes was enough to make me call 911 while screaming out for store security and blocking all customers from leaving the store until my child was brought to me—which she was, about ten Hail Marys and three minutes later.)

The genocide left no one in Rwanda untouched by loss. A million innocent souls lost their lives through the crimes of demented killers. The killers themselves lost their humanity by committing unspeakable atrocities —and many, haunted by their crimes, lost their minds. Virtually everyone who survived the slaughter would discover that they had lost their loved ones, their homes, their possessions, their futures, as well as their faith in both humanity and God.

IN MY MEDITATION I COULD SEE that the Fifth Joyful Mystery is not only about loss. It is joyful because it is about finding something that *was* lost—and of course in this case, it is about finding Jesus. Reflecting on this mystery showed me that virtue can be found in loss, even the unimaginable loss caused by genocide or the countless other wars, pogroms, pestilences, plagues, and natural disasters that have afflicted humankind since being expelled from Eden.

Losing everything brought me face-to-face with the one essential truth of my existence: We can rely on nothing but God. Everything else in the world is fleeting—even the people we love and trust most will die one day, or leave us, or hurt us, or let us down, or betray us. We are all just dust, and to dust we will return. Only God is eternal, and His love is everlasting—that is the only fact we can rely on. It is the only enduring truth in the universe.

So, although I lost everything else when I went into hiding, I had found God's universal truth. More important, though, I knew that if I ever lost sight of the truth, all I'd have to do is keep looking—like Mary and Joseph, sooner or later I would find Jesus. And so I prayed:

> *Dear Father, thank You for sparing me for another day and allowing me to spend time with Mary and Joseph. And thank You for giving me the chance to learn by their example not to give up when I am searching for Jesus, no matter how painful or difficult that search can be. And You know that it is so, so difficult for me right now. I don't know what has happened to my family, and I don't know why You are letting this awful killing go on and on—thousands of us Tutsis must have been murdered, or worse, by now. But I know You must have your reasons . . . maybe we are all supposed to learn some big lessons from this nightmare, and maybe it will bring us closer to You . . . but it is so hard to know if that is true when the killing continues on the other side of the bathroom door.*
>
> *God, please, please, please don't let them find me, don't let me die being ignorant of the purpose for all this pain. And please protect my family . . .*

*or if they have been killed—which please don't let that be the case—take them into your arms right away. I know you are there for me, Father; I feel you all around me when I pray beside Mary . . . but it is hard to feel You near when I stop praying. When my prayers end I see and hear all the wicked, evil things going on around me. Please help me find the strength to keep You in my heart always, so I can find Jesus wherever I look . . . even if I am looking at people who are trying to kill me. And please, God, don't forget to watch over my parents and brothers, wherever they are tonight. Amen.*

# PART III

# THE LUMINOUS MYSTERIES

## (Traditionally Prayed on Thursdays)

# CHAPTER 15

# THE LUMINOUS MYSTERIES

As I mentioned at the beginning of the book, the Luminous Mysteries are not part of the traditional rosary that I grew up praying, or that I carried with me into the bathroom. Earlier I explained that according to Catholic lore, the Blessed Mother presented St. Dominic with the traditional rosary in the Middle Ages as a tool to fight evil and convert hearts. For centuries that rosary remained virtually unchanged and consisted of three five-part Mysteries: the Joyful, the Sorrowful, and the Glorious.

Pope John Paul II, one of the greatest advocates of the Blessed Mother in the 20th century, introduced a new five-part mystery in 2002—these Luminous Mysteries chronicle key moments in Jesus's public ministry, starting from his baptism.

No part of Christ's public ministry, which "illuminated" the world with his truth, is part of the traditional rosary; in his wisdom, John Paul II felt that the addition of these five crucial events in Our Lord's life would bring balance and fullness to the rosary. But the Pope made it clear that it was up to each individual to choose whether or not to include these mysteries, sometimes called the Mysteries of Light, as part of their personal rosary prayers.

I must confess, it took me a long time to warm up to praying this set of mysteries during my daily rosary. So many of my memories were associated with the traditional rosary: praying it with my family in the evening, studying for my test, all the miracles big and small that I'd witnessed over the years while praying it, and the countless life-changing hours spent with my father's beads during the genocide. All of this made me deeply attached to the old-fashioned 15-mystery rosary.

In many ways those traditional prayers became (and remain) a part of my spiritual DNA. But one of the lessons I learned praying the rosary in hiding was to keep our hearts and minds open to receive the word of God in unexpected ways. As my father said to me when I was very young, the rosary is a living prayer. The truth of his words didn't really strike me until I was in hiding and discovered that both prayer *and* faith are organic, living entities that require attention and nourishment to thrive.

So, I am happy to report that reflecting on the Luminous Mysteries is now a regular, rewarding, and much-loved part of my life. This shouldn't have surprised me, not really, considering that the events of Jesus's life covered in the Luminous Mysteries are among my all-time favorite Bible stories. And while I obviously didn't meditate upon them in the same manner as I did with the original 15 mysteries while I was in hiding (since they did not exist as rosary mysteries back then), I certainly *did* reflect on the stories associated with them while I was reading the New Testament whenever I wasn't engaged in active prayer.

I decided to include the Luminous Mysteries in this book because, while they are not technically part of "the prayer that saved my life," their message has always been a part of my daily prayers—as well as the very essence of the faith that forms me as a person.

For obvious reasons, I won't be sharing these mysteries with you in the same fashion that I did the Joyful Mysteries or as I will the Sorrowful and Glorious Mysteries; that is, with Mary by my side as we review certain events in the life of the Blessed Mother and her son. That is not how I meditated upon these stories while I was in hiding. Instead, I will summarize them in a single chapter, much in the way I thought about them while reading my Bible while I was in Pastor Murinzi's bathroom.

I am also putting the Luminous Mysteries in this section of the book because that is where they fit chronologically in the order of biblical events: they follow the Joyful Mysteries and come before the Sorrowful Mysteries. And if you recall from the chapter on my test preparations, learning to put the mystery stories in chronological order was one of the first rosary miracles in my life . . . even if it was just a teensy miracle.

## The First Luminous Mystery: The Baptism of Jesus

When I would read Bible passages about John the Baptist, I'd picture myself standing on the shores of the Jordan River. I saw the waving palm trees and tall reeds that lined the banks and provided this small oasis a bit of shelter against the vast desert, which stretched off into the distance as far as the eye could see.

It is from out of the depths of this wilderness that I imagined hearing the voice of Jesus's cousin, crying out into the hot, dusty wind: "Prepare ye the way of the Lord!"

And then I'd envision John— lean, wiry, bare-chested, and wild-eyed with his passion for God. He was ministering to a long line of Jewish men whom he'd inspired to be baptized to cleanse themselves of sin, prepare for the coming of the Messiah, and begin a new life in God.

John would brush his long beard over his shoulder, take hold of the next waiting supplicant with his strong hands, and sing praises to God as he plunged the startled man under the rippling water. Sometimes he held them beneath the surface so long I thought they would surely drown, which I suppose was the symbolic intention— to die and be reborn in God with all sin washed away.

Occasionally John would shout angrily at the people in line he reckoned had come to be baptized because it made them look pious, or because it was fashionable to be spotted with the popular preacher. He called them phonies, snakes, and liars; he warned these men to repent because they couldn't hide from the approaching truth that was about to change their world forever. But John's anger vanished instantly when those in line parted, and his cousin Jesus stepped forward to be baptized.

Jesus greeted John from the water's edge. He was now a fiercely handsome man of 30, with a dark beard and long, flowing hair that, although covering much of his face, could not conceal the gentle brown eyes he'd inherited from his mother. I pictured him with the same glowing aura that I'd witnessed when I sat with Mary meditating upon the Joyful Mysteries.

John advanced toward Jesus, sank to his knees in the shallow water before him, and cried out for all to hear, "Behold the Lamb of God!" Then he supplicated himself at his cousin's feet, moaning that he was not worthy to tie his sandals, let alone baptize him . . . it was Jesus, John said, who should baptize *him*.

The two men had known each other since they were in their mothers' wombs and were joined by bonds of blood, love, and a supernatural understanding that each of them was playing a role in the greatest story ever told. Now Jesus gently touched John on the shoulder and told him to stand and face him. Then he asked his cousin to baptize him in the name of the Father. He said that it had fallen to John to perform the cleansing ritual that would mark the beginning of Christ's public ministry.

A moment later John carefully lowered his cousin into the Jordan, all the while looking up at the heavens as tears streamed down his face. Tears would often roll down my own cheeks at this point as I realized that the baptismal promises Jesus was making at that moment to God included enduring the horrific torture and crucifixion he would face in three short years.

Yet when John lifted the Lord from beneath the waters, his face was serene. The sky brightened as a dove soared down from heaven, alighting beside Jesus and bathing him in a cloud of brilliant golden light as the Holy Spirit came upon him. Those who stood watching this miraculous event trembled when they heard a voice echo from above, proclaiming: "This is my Son, the beloved, with whom I am well pleased."

This is how the story is described in the Bible:

---

In those days John the Baptist appeared in the wilderness of Judea, proclaiming, "Repent, for the kingdom of heaven has come near." This is the one of whom the prophet Isaiah spoke when he said, "The voice of one crying out in the wilderness: 'Prepare the way of the Lord, make his paths straight.'"

Now John wore clothing of camel's hair with a leather belt around his waist, and his food was locusts and wild honey. Then the people of Jerusalem and all Judea were going out to him, and all the region along the Jordan, and they were baptized by him in the river Jordan, confessing their sins.

But when he saw many Pharisees and Sadducees coming for baptism, he said to them, "You brood of vipers! Who warned you to flee from the wrath to come? Bear fruit worthy of repentance. Do not presume to say to yourselves, 'We have Abraham as our ancestor'; for I tell you, God is able from these stones to raise up children to Abraham. Even now the ax is lying at the root of the trees; every tree therefore that does not bear good fruit is cut down and thrown into the fire.

"I baptize you with water for repentance, but one who is more powerful than I is coming after me; I am not worthy to carry his sandals. He will baptize you with the Holy Spirit and fire. His winnowing fork is in his hand, and he will clear his threshing floor and will gather his wheat into the granary; but the chaff he will burn with unquenchable fire."

Then Jesus came from Galilee to John at the Jordan, to be baptized by him. John would have prevented him, saying, "I need to be baptized by you, and do you come to me?" But Jesus answered him, "Let it be so now; for it is proper for us in this way to fulfill all righteousness." Then he consented. And when Jesus had been baptized, just as he came up from the water, suddenly the heavens were opened to him and he saw the Spirit of God descending like a dove and alighting on him. And a voice from heaven said, "This is my Son, the Beloved, with whom I am well pleased"(Matthew 3:1–17).

After reading the New Testament accounts of Our Lord's baptism I sometimes pondered what my own baptism had meant to me. Of course I couldn't remember the event as I was only an infant at the time, but the duties of being a follower of Jesus were spelled out to me again when I was 12 years old and received the Sacrament of Confirmation.

That's when Father Clement told me that being confirmed made me a soldier for Christ with a duty to defend and spread the message of our faith in word and deed. Reading the description of Jesus emerging from the Jordan already prepared to sacrifice his life for us made me question how dedicated a soldier I was in God's army.

I thought of my father, who offered to lay down his life to defend our neighbors, but pleaded for them not to kill their assailants. That was truly defending the faith in both word and deed. I wished I had Dad's courage.

I thought of the first thing Christ did after his baptism: fasting in the desert for 40 days, where he battled the temptations of the devil. The devil had tempted me while I was in hiding, and I had nearly succumbed to his whispers. I wished I had Christ's strength.

The next time my faith wavered I would remember my father's courage and conviction. And the next time the devil's dark whispering began ringing in my ears, as it always did when I stopped praying, I would recall the message of this passage. So I prayed:

*Dear God, You sent Jesus to be with us, which was a sacrifice for You . . . I can't imagine what it must have felt like to let go of Your only son. And it was a sacrifice for Jesus, who endured so much torment and pain even before he willingly let himself be nailed to the cross for us. His sacrifice and Your sacrifice are examples of Your perfect love for us and of the sacrifices we should all be willing to make for each other.*

*Thank You for showing us the importance of being humble. Jesus was perfect and without sin, but he was baptized like everyone else who wants to begin a life in God—to begin a life with You, Father! And Jesus showed us how important it is to respect and honor Your messengers by bowing down to John and allowing John to baptize him—what humility Jesus showed. Please teach us all to be humble . . . look what we do to each other when we forget humility . . . when we forget that we are all equal in the eyes of the Lord. But we are human, we are blind to the truth, and we play with sin, forgetting that it is like playing with fire and that sometimes we can burn down the world around us and everyone in it.*

*Please watch over my parents and brothers. I know that one day I will be with them again, but please take care of them until I get there. Thank You, Father. Amen.*

## The Second Luminous Mystery: The Wedding at Cana

Most people I know find reading the Bible to be inspirational, spiritually rewarding, morally uplifting, emotionally fulfilling, and even intellectually challenging. But I don't know anyone who describes scripture reading as a good time and lots of fun—and yet, that is exactly what I feel every time I open my Good Book and drink in the atmosphere of my favorite biblical nuptials.

The Wedding at Cana has become one of my favorite mysteries for two reasons. The first is because it highlights an excellent and essential method of praying the rosary. The second reason is that the mystery originates in the Bible passage I most delighted in and enjoyed while in hiding. I have fond memories of the distraction it offered.

As the story opens we find ourselves in the middle of a party. In my mind I always envision a sumptuous banquet in the open courtyard of a large home. The courtyard is filled with tall potted ferns, and dozens of guests sitting at long wooden tables creaking beneath the weight of a score of different delicacies and large chalices of heady wine.

Seated at the center table are Mary and Jesus—both glowing and looking healthy as always, even though Mary has entered middle age and Jesus has embarked on the life of hardship that would be part and parcel of his public ministry. At the next table over are several of Jesus's disciples. They're keeping a close eye on the remarkable man who, with just a few words, had convinced them to abandon their occupations and families to join him on the road to preach love and understanding to the poor and downtrodden.

The wedding feast itself, given the constant economic struggles faced by all but the very rich at the time, must have been a great extravagance for the hosts. Perhaps it was a once-in-a-lifetime celebration that ate up years of savings to celebrate the matrimony of a beloved daughter. At any rate, that's the scenario I choose to imagine, and I believe it was important to the parents of the couple that every guest at their gala affair enjoy themselves and have a good time.

And everyone *is* having the time of their lives, until disaster strikes. In the middle of the party the wine, the lifeblood of the festivities, runs out. Mary, whom I feel had a special bond and kinship with the bride's mother, approaches her son and lets him know about the calamity with the simple, urgently whispered statement: "They have no wine."

Jesus looks at his mother blankly, then, shrugging his shoulders, asks, "What do you want me to do about it, Mother?"

This is followed by one of my favorite exchanges in the Bible, in which I picture Mary fixing her gaze on Jesus and giving him an "I am your mother, young man" look that says, "I know what you can do about it, and you know what you can do about it . . . so, what are you going to do about it?"

Jesus responds by telling her, "My hour has not yet come." I assume what he means by that is the celestial clock has yet to strike the exact preordained moment in time for him to perform his first miracle.

I can't help but think that Mary decides then and there, as thoroughly human as she is, to hurry things along and get her son's ministry completely up and running —because she immediately turns to the servant in charge of the wine and tells him to talk to Jesus about their refreshment problem. I also love thinking that the Blessed Mother knows that Jesus, her darling and dutiful child, loves her as much as she loves him and is incapable of refusing her any request.

Moments later Our Lord performs his first miracle —an act that truly changed the course of history— by instructing household staff to fill six huge jars the size of industrial drums with fresh water, and then miraculously transforming it into the finest wine anyone at the gathering had ever tasted.

The miracle was performed in front of many witnesses, each of whom then spread word of Christ's glory throughout Galilee. Among those witnesses were the disciples that accompanied Mary and Jesus to the wedding and who, if they had any doubts about Jesus when they arrived at the party, became true believers after sampling the wine that helped change the world. And of course, I can only imagine that everyone at the party drank their fill and danced until dawn, and a good time was had by all.

I encourage anyone who has not read this delightful story to take a look at the Bible's depiction:

---

On the third day there was a wedding in Cana of Galilee, and the mother of Jesus was there. Jesus and his disciples had also been invited to the wedding. When the wine gave out, the mother of Jesus said to him, "They have no wine." And Jesus said to her, "Woman, what concern is that to you and to me? My hour has not yet come." His mother said to the servants, "Do whatever he tells you."

Now standing there were six stone water jars for the Jewish rites of purification, each holding twenty or thirty gallons. Jesus said to them, "Fill the jars with water." And they filled them up to the brim. He said to them, "Now draw some out, and take it to the chief steward." So they took it.

When the steward tasted the water that had become wine, and did not know where it came from (though the servants who had drawn the water knew), the steward called the bridegroom and said to him, "Everyone serves the good wine first, and then the inferior wine after the guests have become drunk. But you have kept the good wine until now." Jesus did this, the first of his signs, in Cana of Galilee, and revealed his glory; and his disciples believed in him (John 2:1–11).

---

Every time I read this passage when I was in the bathroom, I was engrossed by the powerful messages interwoven in what first appeared, at least to me, to be a charming and relatively insignificant event. I mean, changing water into wine isn't a trifling matter—it is definitely a miracle and, as such, an act of God, which establishes Jesus as the Son of God. But when I read the story I couldn't help thinking that making wine isn't exactly raising the dead, casting out demons, restoring sight to the blind, or curing any array of horrible illnesses. Still, it is from this "least" of miracles that the fame of Jesus begins to spread.

Second, I was enthralled that it was Mary who initiated the miracle, which made me love and respect her all the more. To know that Jesus listened to his mother and did what she asked, long before he planned to start performing miracles, shows us what impact she had on him, not only then but still today. *Most women,* I thought, *are so often overlooked as they humbly labor quietly behind the scenes, but they are so often the ones responsible for getting things going and getting things done.*

Finally, and most important for me, I recognized how going to Mary is truly a wonderful way of traveling to the heart of Jesus. I would think, *Some of my friends unfamiliar with the rosary think it is silly to pray for Mary to intercede on our behalf, to ask her to ask her son to help us with our problems. They ask, why not just go to Jesus directly? They don't understand that Jesus can't say no to his mom, but they would understand if they read what happened at this wonderful wedding and saw how Mary has the ear, and the heart, of Jesus . . . and that mothers always know best.*

I prayed:

> *Dear Jesus, I have been reading about the first miracle you performed by turning water into wine so*

*people could keep celebrating at the wedding in Cana. It has made my heart so warm seeing the kindness and respect you showed your mom and how much you love her. You appreciated how good she was to you while you were growing up, and you knew how much she loved you so you couldn't say no to her. This is how we should respect our mothers. Thank you for showing us such a good example.*

*This miracle also made me realize how much you are capable of and how much you are willing to do for us to make us happy . . . even if it is just having a good time at a wedding, because those events and rituals can bring us closer to you when we remember all love flows to us from you. Thank you for all the love you give us. Amen.*

## The Third Luminous Mystery: The Proclamation of the Kingdom

If I had been forced to learn the Third Luminous Mystery when I was studying for my rosary test, I think I would have tossed my beads in the air in frustration and set off to find a new method of praying that didn't require so much memorization.

The Proclamation of the Kingdom is a kind of super mystery: it is comprised of all the different Gospel verses related to Jesus urging us to prepare our hearts and souls for heaven, because the Kingdom of God has arrived. It is such a simple proclamation, but it is all encompassing—encapsulating everything Jesus encourages us to do in order to be with him. This is a mystery that cannot be found in just one Bible story or in one Gospel.

To get a full sense of the importance of this one message, we really should read *all* of these verses, each of which touches upon the proclamation and its many implications and manifestations:

Matthew 4:12–22; Matthew 5–7; Matthew 9:9–13; Matthew 13:1–50; Matthew 16:24–28; Matthew 18:1–5; Matthew 18:10–14; Matthew 18:23–35; Matthew 19:13–15; Matthew 20:1–16; Matthew 22:1–14; Mark 1:14–20; Mark 2:13–17; Mark 4:1–32; Mark 8:34–9:1; Mark 10:13–16; Luke 4:16–21; Luke 5:1–11; Luke 5:27–32; Luke 6:20–49; Luke 7:36–50; Luke 8:4–15; Luke 9:23–27; Luke 10:25–37; Luke 12:22–34; Luke 15:1–31; Luke 18:15–17; Luke 19:1–10; John 1:35–51; John 4:1–42; Acts 2:14–42; Acts 9:1–19

As I said, when I was 12 years old and studying for my rosary test, all those passages would have sent me running. But after I passed the test and was hiding for my life in the pastor's bathroom, I turned to these passages to illuminate my path to salvation. It is a righteous path blazed by the words of Jesus Christ, and a path I will follow until my dying day.

These passages all touch upon Christ's call for us to repent, convert, and follow him into the Kingdom of God . . . and they offer us a lifetime of meditation and reflection. But to me, Jesus not only tells us his Kingdom has arrived, he shows us he *is* the Kingdom, and the only way to enter into it is through him.

There are many stories and passages for you to reflect on, but here are a few of my favorites:

— Christ's actual proclamation of the Kingdom's arrival: "The time is fulfilled, and the kingdom of God has come near; repent, and believe in the good news" (Mark 1:15).

— When Jesus commands us to stop thinking of our own needs and wants first and, instead, to take up the cross and follow in his footsteps (Matthew 16:24–28).

— Christ's call to the first disciples (see Matthew 4:18–22; Mark 1:16–20; Luke 5:1–11; and John 1:35–51), and his direction for them to drop their nets and join him to fish for the souls of men.

— There are also the conversion stories, like those of the sinful woman who repents and cries on Jesus's feet (Luke 7:36–50), which gives us a beautiful lesson from Our Lord on the relationship between Christian love and forgiveness. Or take a look at the Sermon on the Mount (Matthew 5–7), where Jesus calls on us to be merciful, love our enemies, and practice the virtues of fasting and almsgiving. He also teaches us how to speak to God in privacy from our heart, and to communicate with Him through the Lord's Prayer. There is also the Sermon on the Plain (Luke 6:20–49), where we are instructed to be generous of heart, not to judge others, and to build our spiritual house on the rock of our faith in God.

Yet if anyone asks me to recommend one single Bible passage to reflect upon while praying the Third Luminous Mystery, I suggest this one, which I think has it covered:

Blessed are the poor in spirit, for theirs is the kingdom of heaven. Blessed are those who mourn, for they will be comforted. Blessed are the meek, for they will inherit the earth. Blessed are those who hunger and thirst for righteousness, for they will be filled. Blessed are the merciful, for they will receive mercy.

Blessed are the pure in heart, for they will see God. Blessed are the peacemakers, for they will be called children of God. Blessed are those who are persecuted for righteousness' sake, for theirs is the kingdom of heaven (Matthew 5:3–10).

———————————————————————————

There is so much in this mystery to reflect upon that I often think of it as a road map containing the directions to heaven with all the safest, most reliable routes highlighted in red. All you have to do if you get lost while traveling the road of life is just pull over to the side, pull out your Bible, and seek direction in the passages describing the Proclamation.

This is my personal prayer concerning the Third Luminous Mystery:

*Dear Jesus, thank you for teaching us how to find you, and for showing us the road to follow to reach the Kingdom of God. During the genocide, I remember always wondering what went wrong—how did people become capable of such evil acts? When I read your words, especially those you spoke while preaching, I realized you had given us directions containing everything we needed to know to live righteous lives and ensure ourselves a place in heaven when we leave this world. People in Rwanda forgot about your directions, and they forgot about your Father's commandments . . . and that is when everything went so horribly wrong. Thank you for loving us so much, and for teaching us how to love. Amen.*

## *The Fourth Luminous Mystery: The Transfiguration*

Painting a picture in my mind of the Bible story from which the Fourth Luminous Mystery originates has never required much imagination on my part. The scene was imprinted on my mind before I learned to read.

When I was very young I was presented with a richly colored and wonderfully illustrated children's Bible. One of the book's most powerful images was its depiction of the Transfiguration, in which we see Jesus—clothed in robes of the purest white, and his golden aura aglow as always—standing high atop a mountain peak while talking to two Old Testament prophets, Moses and Elijah. The trio is bathed in a swirling riot of vivid reds and crimson hues that highlights the brilliance of the white light streaming down from the parting clouds and illuminating both heaven and earth.

All the while, three of Jesus's favorite apostles—Peter, James, and John—are standing on the ground far below, staring up at the miraculous event while shielding their eyes against the blinding Light of God.

As a little girl, I always thought about how wonderful and terrifying it must have been for the apostles to see the raw power and glory of heaven exposed like that right in front of them . . . how marvelous to know without a doubt that heaven was real and right there waiting for you.

It's funny how the human mind works, because the impression I formed of this mystery when I was four years old has basically never changed to this very day. I believed then, as I do now, that the Transfiguration was one of Christ's ways of showing us what lay behind his promises. It is a message from which we all can take heart and in which we can all find faith whenever we read the story in the Bible:

---

Six days later, Jesus took with him Peter and James and his brother John and led them up a high mountain, by themselves. And he was transfigured before them, and his face shone like the sun, and his clothes became dazzling white. Suddenly there appeared to them Moses and Elijah, talking with him. Then Peter said to Jesus, "Lord, it is good for us to be here; if you wish, I will make three dwellings here, one for you, one for Moses, and one for Elijah." While he was still speaking, suddenly a bright cloud overshadowed them, and from the cloud a voice said, "This is my Son, the Beloved; with him I am well pleased; listen to him!" When the disciples heard this, they fell to the ground and were overcome by fear. But Jesus came and touched them, saying, "Get up and do not be afraid." And when they looked up, they saw no one except Jesus himself alone.

As they were coming down the mountain, Jesus ordered them, "Tell no one about the vision until after the Son of Man has been raised from the dead" (Matthew 17:1–9).

---

When I was in hiding, I sometimes would stare up at the little air-vent window at the top of the wall that was our only source of fresh air and natural light. It was covered up at all times with a red cloth, but occasionally I could see though a small hole and make out the sky. The crimson color of the cloth gave the light an eerie shade that reminded me of the Transfiguration picture in my children's Bible.

I imagined that if I stared long and hard enough at that little opening I might see Jesus appear high on a mountaintop with the old prophets. And I was sure that if I asked him to, he would part the clouds for me and peel open the sky to give a glimpse of the beauty and the glory of heaven I so desperately wanted to see—and to show me that paradise really did await me on the other side of my sadness, suffering, and sorrow. So I prayed:

> *Dear Jesus, thank you for showing us your transfiguration. I especially love that you revealed that the glory of God is all around you and just beyond the veil that separates us from heaven, and that if we follow in your footsteps we will see behind the veil one day when we join you in your Kingdom. By showing the apostles this glimpse of heaven, you strengthened their faith so they would not falter in their belief after you left them. After your crucifixion, the apostles went into the world and spread the word of God and built your church—that would never have happened if you had not given them such amazing faith. Please help strengthen my faith as you strengthened theirs so I can serve you as one of your true disciples. Amen.*

## The Fifth Luminous Mystery: The Institution of the Eucharist

If you've ever seen Leonardo da Vinci's famous painting *The Last Supper,* you have witnessed the origins of the final Luminous Mystery. It was at this Passover meal, the final meal Jesus shared with his 12 disciples, that Christ instituted the Sacrament of the Eucharist. I have often thought about the love and pain of that last supper; I am continually amazed by the loving generosity Jesus exhibited when he offered the apostles, and all of us living today, this most incredible gift that allows us all to keep him alive within us.

You see, the meal did not begin well. Unbeknownst to anyone (except Jesus, through divine intuition) Judas had already taken 30 pieces of silver in exchange for betraying Christ. All those sitting at the table beginning the celebratory meal, with the exception of Judas, were stunned when Jesus announced that someone in the group was about to betray him. Can you imagine the uproar, the sick panic those who loved him must have felt realizing they were about to lose him? The shouting that must have erupted, the pointing of fingers, accusations, denials, and finally, the tears?

Our Lord knew he was about to die, that his disciples would scatter in fear when he was crucified, and that even Peter, the rock upon which Christ would build his church, would deny knowing him. Yet he loved them as he loves us, and he knew the apostles would need him after his death. So, after he announced the betrayal, he sat down and demonstrated for the first time in history how those who follow him can always bring him into their bodies, into their hearts, and into their souls. It is a blessed and beautiful custom, and a sacrament that stretches back to the very founding of the church.

I read about the Last Supper just about every day while I was in hiding and never tired of it, partly because of the powerful story; and partly because I had four versions to choose from, either Matthew, Mark, Luke, or John. My personal favorite is below:

So the disciples did as Jesus had directed them, and they prepared the Passover meal.

When it was evening, he took his place with the twelve; and while they were eating, he said, "Truly I tell you, one of you will betray me." And they became greatly distressed and began to say to him one after another, "Surely not I, Lord?" He answered, "The one who has dipped his hand into the bowl with me will betray me. The Son of Man goes as it is written of him, but woe to that one by whom the Son of Man is betrayed! It would have been better for that one not to have been born." Judas, who betrayed him, said, "Surely not I, Rabbi?" He replied, "You have said so."

While they were eating, Jesus took a loaf of bread, and after blessing it he broke it, gave it to the disciples, and said, "Take, eat; this is my body." Then he took a cup, and after giving thanks he gave it to them, saying, "Drink from it, all of you; for this is my blood of the covenant, which is poured out for many for the forgiveness of sins. I tell you, I will never again drink of this fruit of the vine until that day when I drink it new with you in my Father's kingdom."

When they had sung the hymn, they went out to the Mount of Olives (Matthew 26:19–30).

---

During the genocide, one of the greatest challenges I faced in maintaining my faith was being separated from the places and people most involved in my religious life. My parents and brothers, whom I had prayed the rosary with most of my life, were gone from me. The members of the women's prayer group I regularly attended at university were dead, or in hiding like I was. It was obviously impossible for me to attend Mass, sing hymns, or go to weekly confession. I missed all of these terribly, but while

I was in Pastor Murinzi's bathroom, I learned that I could forge an incredible relationship with God armed only with my Bible and rosary. However, there remained one part of my spiritual life that I hungered for as much as I was hungering for food: receiving the Eucharist during Holy Communion.

To put it simply, when I take the blessed bread and wine into my mouth during Communion, I know that I am taking the body and blood of Christ into my own body. Since receiving my First Communion when I was just nine years old, I have always felt the warmth of Our Lord's love envelop my heart the instant I accept the Blessed Sacrament.

The Eucharist is such a part of my connection to Jesus that I would (and often still do) happily spend hours at a time in church on weekday afternoons, whenever the priest would place the consecrated Host upon the altar and invite everyone in the community to sit in the pews and meditate on the meaning of the Eucharist. This beautiful form of worship is known as Adoration of the Eucharist, and there are very few things—other than the rosary and Holy Communion—that make me feel closer to God.

In the bathroom, I would meditate on the Eucharist after reading one of the Bible's accounts of the Last Supper. And then I would say a long prayer of thanks to Jesus for giving us such an incredible way to be with him on Earth before we are in heaven. The Eucharist seemed to me a prayer in itself, so instead of saying "Amen" after sharing my thoughts and thanking God and Jesus as I usually did, I would think about the words of Paul.

After his miraculous conversion on the road to Damascus, Paul began spreading Christ's gospel across the known world. He also taught, to all who would listen, the exact method the disciples learned from the Lord on how to

instantly bring Christ into your body . . . and through
your body, into your heart, and soul, and life:

---

For I received from the Lord what I also handed
on to you, that the Lord Jesus on the night when he
was betrayed took a loaf of bread, and when he had
given thanks, he broke it and said, "This is my body
that is for you. Do this in remembrance of me." In
the same way he took the cup also, after supper, saying, "This cup is the new covenant in my blood. Do
this, as often as you drink it, in remembrance of me"
(1 Corinthians 11:23–25).

---

# PART IV

# THE SORROWFUL MYSTERIES

(Traditionally Prayed on Tuesdays and Fridays)

# CHAPTER 16

# THE FIRST SORROWFUL MYSTERY

## The Agony in the Garden

Meditating on the Sorrowful Mysteries was not easy for me during the genocide. The five events that they chronicle in Christ's life depict his mental anguish, public humiliation, brutal beating, and torture, all culminating in his sadistic execution on the cross. Focusing on some of the earlier mysteries had provided me with spiritual inspiration, renewed faith, and wonderfully happy moments of companionship with the Blessed Mother—as well as a welcomed and much-needed escape from the horror of the genocide that roared around me like a relentless cyclone of evil.

Taking the rosary in my hand and realizing that I was about to see Jesus subjected to the very same barbaric acts being perpetrated against my friends and neighbors was almost too much for me. Not only did my mind recoil from witnessing more violence inflicted on yet another innocent victim—perhaps the most innocent in history—but also my heart broke into a thousand pieces when I imagined sitting with my head in Mary's lap as she watched her child flayed alive and then nailed to a cross. How could I comfort my comforter? How could I ease her pain when my own was so overwhelming?

If not for the rising whisper of the devil's voice in my ear and the arrival of a band of killers at Pastor Murinzi's front door, I may never have completed a single one of the Sorrowful Mysteries. And what an incredible loss that would have been for me. Yes, I would have avoided having to contemplate horrific and vicious acts committed against our Lord—but I would also have missed out on many hours of deep meditation upon crucial episodes in the life of Christ, as well as the story of our salvation.

As you shall read in the pages that follow, it's doubtful that, had I skipped over the Sorrowful Mysteries, I ever would have learned the lessons I needed to learn to evade the devil's grasp, such as how to let go of my anger or how to forgive. Most likely, I would have eventually stood up, kicked open the bathroom door, and thrown myself at the killers so they'd put me out of my misery once and for all. But as the killers approached our hideout on this particular day, my fear outweighed all other concerns. I quickly crossed myself, embraced the rosary's opening prayers, and announced my intention to meditate on the First Sorrowful Mystery.

Once again I was in the lap of the Blessed Mother; there were no killers at the door, no devil in my ear, and no fear in my heart. There was only the sweet comfort of a loving mother's hand on my head. Suddenly it was dark, and I shivered as the temperature dropped. My face was moistened with rising dew, and I detected the sweet fragrance of jasmine and the earthy aroma of figs. A thousand stars appeared in the night sky, revealing a grassy slope on the edge of a stand of olive trees.

About a dozen or so men emerged from the shadows of the trees and started walking up the hill. The man at the front of the group raised his hand and signaled for all but a few to go back, then the smaller group came up the slope toward us. Even in the dim, hazy light cast by the stars, this man stood out. I recognized him immediately by the glowing golden aura—although dimmer now —that I had always associated with Jesus. His handsome face appeared older, even older than his 33 years. He looked weary and worried, and his shoulders slumped as he turned and talked to the three men he had brought with him. Through my scripture reading, I knew who they were: the cherished disciples Peter, James, and John. I also knew what Jesus was asking of them: to stay awake and pray while he went off to pray alone.

It was the evening of the Passover meal, during which Jesus had announced his betrayal and initiated the Eucharist in front of the apostles. Christ knew that his ministry was at an end and his death was at hand. After the Last Supper he had come here, to the Garden of Gethsemane, a favorite prayerful retreat, as he desperately needed to meditate and talk to his Father about what was about to occur.

Jesus walked a few yards away from his companions and knelt to pray. I could see that his hands were trembling, and he seemed barely able to raise his head toward heaven. I imagined he was now carrying on his shoulders the sins of every human who had ever been born, along with the sins of every person who ever would be born. It was remarkable that he wasn't crushed beneath the accumulated wickedness.

He began to pray but stopped and walked back to his disciples, who had fallen asleep. His face was pained as he woke them and asked why they could not keep him company for just an hour, the one hour he truly needed a friend. But the disciples, despite promising to stay awake and pray, fell asleep the moment he walked away. He would come back to them once more with the same sad result—he was truly alone in the world.

I thought I heard a moan of grief pass through the Blessed Mother's lips, but she would not let me turn to look at her, gently holding my head and stroking my hair as her son pleaded with God to give him a way to avoid the fate awaiting him.

Jesus got to his feet and raised his hands to heaven, and then he flung himself onto the ground. He called on God again, getting to his knees and gasping as he prayed, as though he were drowning in the air he breathed. He wept; beads of blood appeared on his forehead and streamed down his cheeks as he asked God one more time to take the cup of pain from his lips. His anguish was so human, my heart poured out to him.

I could see at this moment that Jesus was a man, a person like me, and like me he did not want to die at the hands of vicious killers who cared nothing about the love in his heart or the kindness in his soul. Then he slowly turned his face to heaven, and Our Lord's golden aura brightened as his anguished expression transformed into one of acceptance.

EACH OF THE FOUR GOSPELS has an account of what happened in the Garden of Gethsemane, but this is the one I read most often in hiding:

They went to a place called Gethsemane; and he said to his disciples, "Sit here while I pray." He took with him Peter and James and John, and began to be distressed and agitated. And he said to them, "I am deeply grieved, even to death; remain here, and keep awake." And going a little farther, he threw himself on the ground and prayed that, if it were possible, the hour might pass from him. He said, "Abba, Father, for you all things are possible; remove this cup from me; yet, not what I want, but what you want" (Mark 14:32–36).

---

Reflecting on the biblical accounts of this event affected me profoundly while I struggled with my own pain, doubt, and crisis of faith in the bathroom. As I mentioned previously, at first I avoided the Sorrowful Mysteries for fear of accentuating my own suffering by adding on the suffering of Jesus and Mary.

I reasoned that if I wanted more agony and terror, I needed only to peek through the tiny bathroom window and behold a world where human butchery had become the norm. No, I reasoned it was best for my fragile emotional and mental state to meditate only on mysteries and stories featuring an overjoyed and radiant expectant Mary or an adorable baby Jesus, or to read about a happy wedding where everyone's cup overflowed with incredible wine.

However, when my fear finally drove me to meditate on the Sorrowful Mysteries, I discovered that reflecting on Christ's pain and anguish didn't add to my own woes; instead, it put them in perspective. Like me, Jesus didn't want to die violently, and he wanted to escape the excruciating pain awaiting him. So he got on to his knees and begged God to make it all go away.

In the Garden of Gethsemane Jesus seemed fully human to me, making me love him all the more and allowing me to readily identify with his perfectly understandable moment of human weakness. It seemed that during his dark hour in the Garden, Christ wasn't thinking of cleansing the sins of the world; he was thinking of a way to escape an agonizing death.

But as I meditated more deeply, I came to believe this story is referred to as his Agony in the Garden because Christ feared the pain of crucifixion. I believe his true suffering arose from the battle raging within him—the war between his divine self, who had come to save mankind, and his human self, who wanted to live free of pain.

For me, lying on the bathroom floor and using all my powers of prayer to save my own skin, everything clicked into sharp and sudden focus. I realized that the moment Our Lord yielded to his higher self, his mental agony ended. In that act of surrender to a higher power, Jesus simply did what he knew he had to: he did the right thing by submitting to and doing God's will, not his own. Although he would endure suffering beyond belief in the hours to come, he would fulfill his destiny and his obligation and promise to God, and, in the process, deliver mankind from the tortures of the damned.

IN THIS, MY FIRST TRULY DEEP MEDITATION upon a Sorrowful Mystery, I had set foot on a new path of spiritual growth. Although I had been praying incessantly since entering the bathroom and delving deeper and deeper into the Joyful and Glorious Mysteries, I had ignored the instructive pain that is woven throughout the Sorrowful Mysteries, a pain that would prove unexpectedly and even miraculously liberating.

I began to see that when we come to God in prayer only when we seek relief from our own suffering, we are forever asking God what He can do for us, not asking God what we can do for Him—which is where real spiritual growth begins.

And so I prayed:

*Dear Father, thank You for sending Jesus to deliver us from our own sin and wickedness . . . I am just coming to understand now how really, really wicked we humans can be to each other and to ourselves.*

*I can only imagine what Christ must have felt like carrying all that evil with him to his crucifixion. His pain must have been unbearable, and I understand much better now what he must have gone through in the Garden of Gethsemane. His soul was so pure, and yet he had to take on so much evil.*

*What would I do if You asked me to take the darkness of all the evil of this genocide into my own heart so that others would not die with those terrible sins on their souls . . . and then what would I do if You then asked to let the very people committing those sins strip me in public, beat me with whips, nail me to a cross, and laugh at me while they watched me die a slow and agonizing death?*

*If I am honest, I don't think I would be brave enough to say yes to You!*

*That is why I am asking You to forgive me for being so selfish during our talks. It seems I am always asking You to help me, and I don't really ask what You need from me. I still want You to save me from these killers; there is no sense in lying to You about that because you know everything anyway.*

*But I want to be of service to You, Father, so please give me the strength to say, as Jesus said in the Garden: "Thy will be done, not mine." Amen.*

---

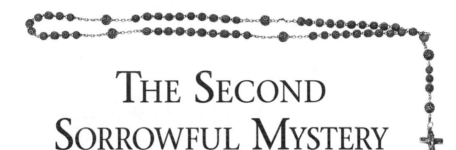

# CHAPTER 17

# THE SECOND SORROWFUL MYSTERY

## The Scourging at the Pillar

There are few passages in the Bible more distressing than these eight words from the Gospel of John: *Then Pilate took Jesus and had him flogged.*

I have never seen a person being flogged, but I knew someone who saw it happen during the genocide—and their description of the noise, blood, and tearing flesh is something I wished I'd never heard. And if you have ever seen Mel Gibson's *The Passion of the Christ*, you also have an excellent and all-too-graphic image of what those eight words from John meant for Our Lord.

I dreaded going to Our Lady's side to meditate upon a mystery in which she would be forced to endure a sight too terrible for a mother's heart to bear. But the Blessed Mother had been with me and guided me during my meditation of the first Sorrowful Mystery, and it is thanks to her that I discovered how rich spiritual fruit can be when it comes through a painful lesson. So no matter how unendurable it may have seemed to me to dwell and reflect upon Christ's scourging, I knew the Blessed Mother would want me at her side to learn all there was to learn from her child's suffering.

So, with my father's red-and-white beads in hand, I began my introductory prayers. I made the Sign of the Cross while invoking the name of the Father, Son, and Holy Spirit; reaffirmed my faith through the Apostles' Creed; greeted and praised God while seeking His guidance and protection with the Lord's Prayer; summoned to mind the grace and beauty of the Blessed Mother while saying three Hail Marys; celebrated the splendor of the heavenly host praying the Glory Be; and then said one more Our Father, asking for my sins to be pardoned. Finally, I asked to be spared the agonies of hell, that the killers' hearts be converted, and for the souls of their victims to be whisked immediately into heaven by reciting the Fátima Prayer. Feeling my heart rate slow and stress level plummet, I announced my intention to meditate on the Second Sorrowful Mystery.

Again I was with Mary, and we immediately found ourselves in a dark, cavernous room crowded with shouting men. They stood in a semicircle before a seated official who wore a long, lavishly adorned smock and a pointy, gold-colored hat reminiscent of a pope's miter. Suddenly Jesus was pushed into the room and knocked to the floor, falling at the feet of the man in the gold hat. I knew this must be the high priest, and that he and his cohorts wanted Jesus dead because his words gave hope to the downtrodden and threatened their own power.

The room erupted with cheers as the high priest handed down a death sentence to Our Lord, ordering that he be taken to the Roman prefect, who alone had the authority to carry out the execution. Jesus was being manhandled out of the room when the scene shifted to a dusty courtyard in front of palatial white-marbled building, framed by a dozen stately pillars. Hundreds of people packed the yard, hissing insults and shouting out for Christ's death. Several Roman soldiers shielded Jesus from the angry gathering while marching him toward the wide stone steps leading up to the palace.

Above this scene, striding back and forth across the palace's porch, was the Roman prefect of Judea, Pontius Pilate. He was barking at the mob that he could find no fault in Jesus and would not execute an innocent man—but the mob roared for Christ's death. Pilate offered to execute the notorious thief Barabbas as a substitute to satisfy its blood lust, but the mob would not be satisfied with this and grew even angrier.

At last Pilate gave the maddened crowd what they wanted, and more. He famously announced that he would wash his hands of Christ's blood and ordered Jesus to be executed, but not before he received a thorough scourging: a flogging with a whip made of multiple leather strips, to which flesh-tearing bits of jagged bone and metal had been attached. Through trial and error Roman soldiers had discovered that 40 lashes with this merciless weapon would prove fatal, so the limit of lashes per prisoner was set at 39—and that is what Jesus received.

Mary and I watched as Jesus was tied to a large stone pillar in the center of the courtyard and stripped of his cloak. Both of us recoiled at the first harsh crack of the whip, and the Blessed Mother moaned when the lash ripped through the skin of her beloved son's back.

I turned my head away and buried my face into Mary's lap, but I still heard the *crack, crack, crack* of the whip as it was pulled back and released again and again through Christ's ruined flesh. In my heart I kept crying out: "Why doesn't he just make them stop?!" I felt tears streaming down my face, and I didn't know if they were Mary's or my own. Although my head was turned and my eyes closed, the image of what was being done to Our Lord continued to play in my mind. I intuitively knew that because I had come to the Blessed Virgin in prayer to understand this mystery, she was not letting me escape the brutal lesson I needed to learn.

When the vicious whipping finally ended at last, the image of Christ's crumpled body loomed in my thoughts. His flesh hung in chunks from his rib cage, shards of broken bone poked through his chest, and he was completely drenched in blood. I did not recognize him as a man, and I could not look for a second longer. I begged Mary to stop . . . I had seen enough.

SADLY, THIS WAS ONLY THE BEGINNING. Pilate would soon dispatch the battered and broken Messiah to his final journey toward Calvary, as recounted in the Bible:

> So when Pilate saw that he could do nothing, but rather that a riot was beginning, he took some water and washed his hands before the crowd, saying, "I am innocent of this man's blood; see to it yourselves." Then the people as a whole answered, "His blood be on us and on our children!" So he released Barabbas for them; and after flogging Jesus, he handed him over to be crucified (Matthew 27:24–26).

Reflecting on this horrendous assault upon Our Lord has on occasion made me physically ill. The images of a battered Jesus still haunt me today if I linger too long on the Second Sorrowful Mystery. When I was in hiding and contemplating the meaning of Christ's bloodied and torn flesh, I kept remembering the words of Father Clement during a sermon he had given years before, in which he encouraged everyone, and particularly the youngsters in the congregation, to avoid the sins of the flesh. He said, "Christ died for our sins of the flesh, so do not make his monumental sacrifice meaningless by making the purpose of your life a pursuit for carnal satisfaction or by turning your body into a palace of fleshly delights."

I was a bit young to appreciate what that sermon meant back then, but I grew to understand the importance of purity and of not becoming obsessed with the pleasures of the flesh. My thoughts on that while in hiding were this: *Once we cave in to some desire, we can lose all sight of what is right and important. All I have to do is press my ear to the wall to understand that.* Outside the bathroom I often heard the killers talking about the pleasure they'd been taking in both the rape and murder of women they used to know and treat with respect—I could see how men who were once decent had developed a taste for wickedness. Sin may start small, but it can catch up with us and pull us down.

As I REFLECTED MORE ON THIS MYSTERY I pondered the many levels of humiliation Our Lord endured even before being tied to the pillar. He was first betrayed by Judas; and while suffering through his dark night of the soul in the Garden of Gethsemane, he was abandoned by his disciples who would not stay awake with him, including Peter, who later denied Christ. He was falsely accused of crimes; roughed up, shoved, mocked, and insulted; sentenced to death; and beaten to within an inch of his life.

And yet Jesus never stopped the brutality, although he had the power to bring Pilate's palace tumbling to the ground. He never insulted or belittled his accusers—not those who condemned him, or the people in the crowd, or even the soldier who scourged him.

For me this seemed to be a lesson in humility, enduring the pain of life, and self-sacrifice for a greater good or higher purpose. Lessons I would carry with me when I left the bathroom and keep close to my heart for the rest of my life. So I prayed:

> *Dear God, thank You for the sacrifices Jesus made for us during his time on Earth. He bore everything that was done to him with humility, grace, and love. Even though he was spit on and beaten, he continued to love us right up to the second he died. What amazes me is that he really could have stopped the beatings and stopped the pain—the only power his tormentors had over him was the power he allowed them to have. He gave us an example of how to endure pain without losing our humanity. Many of us who are hurt by others want to strike out and hurt them back—I know I do, God. But I want to be able to do what Jesus wants us to do . . . carry our pain without bitterness and be thoughtful of others, even those who hurt us.*

> *Please give me the courage to withstand the suffering I encounter in this life. If it is Your will that I go through this hardship, I will do it as graciously as I can manage, but You and I both know I have not been managing that well up to now . . . I still have much anger and hatred, and no matter how hard I try, it is still there in a corner of my heart and comes over me without my permission. I continue to ask You to show me how to rid myself of this bitter disease of anger.*

*And God, I see how Jesus's purity never wavered, even when his flesh was being ripped from his body. He remained constant always, in word and deed. Help me find the strength to keep my thoughts, deeds, words, and intentions always pure. I can see what happens to people—to the world—if they let their hearts stray from You and then choose to satisfy whatever urge that sweeps across them. Please spare me from being found in this bathroom by a man like that . . . I beg You to just take me into Your arms before letting that happen to me, Your humble servant.*

*I ask You also to remember to look out for my parents, who are also Your true servants; and my brothers, who are living chaste and pure lives in honor of You and Your Son. Watch over them, God. Amen.*

# CHAPTER 18

# THE THIRD
# SORROWFUL MYSTERY

## The Crowning of Thorns

As soon as I announced my intention to meditate on the Third Sorrowful Mystery, I was thrust back into the same appalling scenario from which I had just escaped. Jesus, his arms still bound to the pillar, sagged against the rough stone in a semiconscious stupor. Long strips of crimson flesh dangled from his body like the remnants of a shredded shirt.

The soldier who had flogged Our Lord with such vicious proficiency dropped his whip and drew his short sword as he advanced on his victim. With a swift flick of his blade, he cut the ropes binding Jesus to the pillar . . . and then he lifted his leg to the height of his waist and drove his heavy boot into Christ's side.

Once again I buried my face into Mary's lap as her son was sent sprawling onto the rocky ground face-first. My ears hurt from the roar of the vengeful mob cheering wickedly as Jesus huddled against the earth. They began chanting, "Kill him, kill him, kill him"—in the exact same way that the Hutu killers chanted their hunting songs while searching Pastor Murinzi's house looking for Tutsis to murder.

I clasped my head in my hands to block the horrible howling, unsure if the shouts were coming from Pilate's courtyard or the pastor's backyard. Then I heard Mary's soft, sad voice firmly instructing me to "Behold my son, your Lord." As soon as she held my hands in hers, my fear evaporated. Lifting my face from her lap, I turned my eyes once again toward her suffering son.

The soldiers were drunk with the smell of blood and high on the approval of the mob. One of them pulled Jesus up by his hair while another roughly spun him around and draped a purple robe across his bloody shoulders. The other soldiers laughed, because purple is the color of kings. The soldier who had flogged Jesus now began dragging him across the courtyard, parading him before the mob and shouting to them, "Salute your sovereign; bow to your king; all hail the King of Jews!"

Another soldier came up from behind while displaying a wreath of thorny vines he'd tied into the shape of a crown. The thorns were at least three inches long, longer than any I had ever seen in the forests or jungles of my African homeland. I shivered as he announced it was time for a coronation—after which he pushed Jesus onto his knees, and then planted the crown of thorns on his head with all his might. The others laughed and jeered and spit on Christ as the soldier twisted the crown around Our Lord's forehead as though trying to tighten a screw. Blood spurted from a dozen puncture wounds and lacerations on his head and brow.

The soldiers held Jesus up before the cackling crowd one more time, and the courtyard echoed with a two-word demand: "Crucify him."

I sobbed uncontrollably into Mary's lap, but this time I did not turn away. Through my tears I became transfixed by the expression on Christ's face. The prolonged and excruciatingly painful torture I had just witnessed being inflicted upon him was far beyond what any man could endure. Yet that is exactly what I saw standing before me: I saw Jesus as a man in full. He was the mightiest force in the universe, but upon his face I saw no sign of an all-powerful deity who could or would smite down his enemies for their vicious and unjust behavior.

There was something else, something I *didn't* see, that enthralled me even more. While Our Lord's physical agony was seared across his features, there was no trace of anger, malice, or hatred. He'd been beaten, broken, degraded, and humiliated; but to my eyes, the more they attempted to dehumanize him, the more truly human he became. Jesus had chosen to be among us, not about us. Because we cannot avoid suffering, he accepted his suffering in order to bond with us completely.

The golden aura I had always seen around Jesus during my meditations was no longer there, but what I *did* see was an incredible nobility of spirit radiating from his bleeding, battered body. Christ had just shown me what it meant to face suffering with dignity, courage, and grace—qualities that, while perhaps not divine, were sublimely human.

The crowd's cries for crucifixion escalated, and the soldiers tore the robe from Our Lord's back along with much of his flayed skin. As they yanked him to the palace gate to fetch the cross they would soon nail him to, he took a last look at the jeering mob. There were tears rolling down his cheeks, but I don't think they were from the pain of his wounds. I recognized the look on his face as he stared at the hateful people whom he loved so much that he was about to die for them. I could see that his feelings were what had truly been hurt.

ALL FOUR GOSPELS INCLUDE a version of this part of Christ's torture. I am partial to this one, however:

---

> And they clothed him in a purple cloak; and after twisting some thorns into a crown, they put it on him. And they began saluting him, "Hail, King of the Jews!" They struck his head with a reed, spat upon him, and knelt down in homage to him. After mocking him, they stripped him of the purple cloak and put his own clothes on him. Then they led him out to crucify him (Mark 15:17–20).

---

One of the most terrifying and incomprehensible aspects of the genocide I grappled with while in hiding was how people I had loved, and who had loved me, my entire life had suddenly turned into creatures I no longer recognized. Even worse than not recognizing them was knowing that they could not and would not recognize *me*. They no longer saw me as Immaculée, the next-door neighbor, the babysitter, the best friend, the Sunday-school teacher, or the beloved daughter of Leonard and Rose. What these people I had loved like family saw when they looked at me now was a cockroach, a snake that had to be killed. They saw me as subhuman.

The first time this really hit home was when I arrived at Pastor Murinzi's house after the killing had started. When I entered his home the pastor was entertaining several guests in his living room, all of whom I had known for years, including one of my oldest and dearest girlfriends. As I moved from person to person offering my hand in greeting, each one refused to extend their hand to me in return or to meet my eyes, unless it was with a look of disgust. Even my oldest friend rebuffed me and treated me worse than she would have a stranger.

In many ways this event affected me more than the death and destruction I experienced. No matter how long or hard I thought about it, I could not understand how people who had once loved me could stop loving me overnight. I was the same caring person I had always been, and the pain of their rejection made me question and doubt the authenticity of every relationship I had ever had and every bit of love I had ever offered or accepted.

It wasn't until I saw the tears on Our Lord's face as he stood before the mob wearing his crown of thorns that I began to understand that pain. The feeling expressed on Jesus's face was the same feeling that took root in my heart that day in the pastor's living room. When so many people who know you well tell you that you are subhuman and worthless, you begin to wonder if they're right, that you really are unlovable. There is no pain more bitter than being rejected by a loved one.

As I REFLECTED MORE UPON THAT SCENE in Pilate's courtyard, I could see that Jesus had fully embraced his humanity, but the soldiers and angry mob had completely lost theirs. And I could see that the people in the pastor's living room had also surrendered their humanity to the dark forces that now ruled Rwanda. To rid myself of the pain of rejection, all I had to do was what Christ had done: have courage in the face of hatred, accept suffering with dignity, and hold on to my God-given humanity even when others had abandoned theirs.

My love and appreciation of Christ swelled at that moment, and I felt much of the confusion and hurt I had been harboring leave my heart. So I prayed:

*Dear God, thank You for easing my heart and showing me through Jesus's love of man what kind of person You want us to be. I mean, who else but Jesus would still feel love for people who hurt him so badly, who spit on him, laughed at him, and threw the love he gave them back in his face? You know that a lot of people whom I have given so much of my love to have rejected me . . . some of them, dear God, are outside the house hunting for me right now . . . I heard them call my name and say they want to kill me. Please don't let that happen!*

*But if they do find me, help me have the courage and love that Your son had when they got their hands on him. He didn't curse them, he didn't threaten them, or hit them with a lightning bolt . . . he endured the pain and he never stopped loving them . . . he never stopped being what a man should be, at least the kind of man that You can be proud of, Father. Maybe, with Your help, I can start to forgive my friends for treating me so poorly . . . but I can't say the same thing about the killers. I hate them. Please forgive me for that—it's a sin, I know, but unless You take that anger from me, I don't know how it will ever go away. I am too weak to forgive them . . . I can't do it on my own.*

*Please watch over my family tonight, wherever they may be. Amen.*

# CHAPTER 19

# THE FOURTH SORROWFUL MYSTERY

## The Carrying of the Cross

Fear of pain prevented me from meditating on the Sorrowful Mysteries when I first went into hiding, and fear of disappointing Mary prompted me to start reflecting on them. However, it was love that opened my hand to pick up the rosary beads and embrace the Fourth Sorrowful Mystery. While I knew that the fourth mystery would be as harrowing as the first, second, and third, something had shifted in me. The pain I was afraid to face by reflecting on Christ's torment had, contrary to all my expectations, helped me face my own pain and fear.

With the Blessed Mother at my side to comfort and guide me, I had explored Our Lord's wretched ordeal more intensely than I had ever done before. Scales had fallen from my eyes, and I was really seeing both sides of Jesus's nature for the first time: the divine and the human. The lessons I was learning by reflecting on both had touched something deep within me. I could feel myself changing, and I felt the devil's hold on me loosen as my fear and terror diminished.

I knew why this was happening. I was feeling the love Christ had for me—for all of us—in an entirely new way. I had experienced a kind of love story happening with the Bible, God, Mary, and Jesus my entire life—a wonderful, pure, and rewarding love story that filled my heart with joy and optimism. But in the pastor's bathroom, I saw that it had been a young, juvenile love—neither mature nor strong enough to weather the storm of a genocide or deep crisis of faith.

I thanked God that my father had handed me his rosary as I left home that last time. Those beads had allowed me to see Jesus as I never had, and my juvenile religious passion had transformed into a relationship with God that was deeper than I could ever have dreamed possible. This was a love so profoundly spiritual that even now my eyes well up searching for words to describe it—only to realize that words fail me. In truth, I didn't know what was happening to me except that I felt I was falling in love with God.

As I began reciting the opening prayers my mind drifted to a lyric from a children's song that a visiting European nun taught us at grammar school: *Jesus loves me, this I know, for the Bible tells me so . . .*

Without realizing it, I had announced the Fourth Sorrowful Mystery . . . and all the warm and fuzzy feelings I had been mulling over vanished as I watched a Roman soldier's boot smash into the back of Jesus's skull.

The shock of it sent my mind reeling and my stomach lurching. For a moment I didn't know where I was, but the calming touch of Mary's hand assured me that I was where I was supposed to be: in the safety and shelter of her lap. The Blessed Mother's loving presence was all around me, yet my eyes couldn't help but note the tortured expression on her face as the scene unfolded before us.

Mary was among a chorus of wailing followers lining the road leading to Calvary, the hill upon which Christ was destined to die. Their keening filled the shallow valley beyond Jerusalem's tall stone walls and echoed up toward heaven.

That's when I saw Jesus, pinned beneath the weight of his enormous wooden cross. As he struggled, Roman soldiers standing at his side kicked him savagely for not moving more quickly. Mary tried to reach out to her beaten, broken, and exhausted son; when a soldier went to shove her away, she was pulled into the crowd by a woman I assumed to be Mary Magdalene.

Jesus got to his feet, hefting the weight of his cross onto his right shoulder, through which a shard of bloodied, broken bone protruded. Any part of his body not concealed by cloth bore the raw, gaping wounds of his recent scourging. The holes punctured into his scalp by the thick thorns of his crown oozed blood; his eye sockets were swollen, caked, and bruised.

A woman stepped into the road, removed her veil, and wiped the blood from his eyes and brow. Her name was Veronica, and her kindness would one day lead her to sainthood—and her veil would forever bear the face of Christ. Her selfless gesture in defiance of the ruthless soldiers moved Jesus deeply. It was the only time since his torment began in the Garden that I saw even a flicker of a smile cross his swollen lips. The soldiers came at Veronica as Our Lord fell again beneath his cross. Mary pushed her way through the crowd and knelt by her boy's side, and he lifted his head from the dirt to face her. It was the first time they had looked into each other's eyes since he'd been arrested.

As I watched on helplessly, I felt my heart swell and expand like a balloon; then the air left my lungs, forcing me to gulp for oxygen. I tried to calm myself but burst into a deep fit of uncontrollable sobs. I wanted to break my meditation, to open my eyes and return to the horrid bathroom . . . to be anywhere but here, watching this unbearable image of a mother's heartache and a son's grieving farewell to her.

I thought of my own mother, then of my father and brothers—and of the likelihood that they could be suffering just as much at this very moment. My panic rose, and I feared that I would suffocate or drown in my own tears. Then the Blessed Mother's voice said, "Behold my son, your Lord." I looked back to the road to see the weeping Mary raise her hand and gently press it against Jesus's cheek. And I felt her hand on *my* cheek. My lungs filled with air and my chest relaxed, but my tears still flowed freely.

The gut-wrenching encounter between mother and son ended abruptly when a soldier stepped between them. Christ, buoyed by his mother's loving touch, got to his feet and pushed himself up the hill. Mary remained kneeling in the dust, her eyes following her boy as he staggered another dozen steps toward death before falling beneath the weight of his cross once again.

THERE ARE SEVERAL ACCOUNTS of Our Lord's arduous journey to Calvary. Yet I often turn to a passage that, with a couple of sentences, says so much:

Then he handed him over to them to be crucified. So they took Jesus; and carrying the cross by himself, he went out to what is called The Place of the Skull, which in Hebrew is called Golgotha (John 19:16–17).

---

Sometimes I feel that I have never stopped meditating on this mystery, which to me embodies the one lesson we need to survive in a world that is so often inexplicably cruel and unjust: we must pick up the cross we have been given to bear and carry on.

Jesus offers us the perfect example of perseverance in the face of adversity. He is purely human as he stumbles along that road and travels his final pilgrimage to crucifixion, armed only with his faith and the knowledge that he is loved by the heavenly Father.

All of us will encounter cruelty, suffering, and heartache on our journey through life—that comes with being human. What matters is how we deal with the troubles we encounter. We can give up and give in to what the world throws at us, or we can do what Jesus did: hold on to our faith, pick up our cross, and carry on along the narrow road to heaven.

DURING MY FIRST WEEKS IN HIDING there seemed to be no end to the obstacles blocking my path to God. I was hunted by devils beyond the bathroom walls and battled with demons within my own mind. Satan whispered lies and promises in my left ear, and the screams of murdered Tutsis echoed in my right. I was starving to death and thought I was bordering on madness. Yet opening my Bible—and my heart—while I prayed the rosary allowed me to forge a faith and love of God that chased the demons from my mind and the hatred from my soul.

As long as I was willing to pick up my cross and take a step toward Jesus, I knew I was stepping toward salvation, as Christ had done. So I prayed:

*Dear God, thank You for never abandoning me when my faith wavered, and thank You for being there for me when there is no one else for me to turn to for protection and guidance. I have always believed in You and in Jesus, but somehow never understood exactly how much You both loved me until I had lost everything. The Blessed Mother has shown me so much through the mysteries, and I see now that you didn't just send Jesus to Earth to preach to us . . . You sent him to Earth to be one of us, to be a human in every way so that he would teach us how to live and how to suffer with dignity, so we can find our way to You by following his example.*

*Oh God, Your son experienced so much cruelty but chose to remain as a lamb among lions. His kindness and sacrifice makes me cry. I never knew someone could love another person so much that they would willingly let themselves be so badly abused—except maybe my dad and mom. But that is what Your son did for us, isn't it, God? That is what Jesus did for me . . . I really see that now like never before. Thank You for showing me such love, and for showing me how much Jesus loves me. I love You both more than ever . . . like it's something brand new. And, of course, I love Mary, too; she is my mom, so it goes without saying.*

*Please watch over my family wherever they are tonight. Amen.*

# CHAPTER 20

# THE FIFTH
# SORROWFUL MYSTERY

## The Crucifixion

There is perhaps no mystery more familiar to people around the world than the Fifth Sorrowful Mystery. I think that, other than among the few remaining deep-forest tribes untouched by modern civilization, it would be difficult to find someone who's never at least seen the iconic image of the Crucifixion. And yet I often wonder, of all those billions of people, how many are intimately familiar with the story or the magnitude of what happened upon that cross so long ago.

As for me, I was sure I knew everything there was to know about the Crucifixion—that is, until I found myself hiding for my life in the bathroom praying with the rosary. With the meditative power of those red-and-white beads, I was able to focus my mind with complete clarity on the meaning of Christ's final words and behavior during the last hours of his life.

After presenting my heart to God through my opening prayers, I was once more sitting at the feet of the Queen of Heaven. A distant hilltop gradually became illuminated beneath the purplish light of a gloomy midmorning sun. Mary had patiently instructed me during my other meditations not to turn away from the suffering I witnessed— I needed to see the pain endured by Our Lord, and by Mary herself, in order to appreciate and understand the depth of Christ's love and sacrifice, as well as the strength of the Blessed Mother.

But the suffering I was to witness now was intolerable. Before me I saw Jesus, beaten nearly beyond recognition and dangling from a rope lassoed around his chest. He was suspended a foot above the ground and swaying in front of the cross he had been forced to carry to Calvary. Several burly Roman soldiers stood on ladders leaning against the back of the cross and worked as a team to quickly pull him up to the crossbeam, where they spread his arms and lashed him to the horizontal wooden beam. One of the soldiers tacked a sign to the cross over Our Lord's head that read: JESUS OF NAZARETH, THE KING OF THE JEWS. He cursed Christ's name as he came down the ladder after cutting his hand on the razor-sharp thorns of Jesus's crown. The ladders were quickly repositioned and, with military efficiency, two soldiers scrambled up on either side of Jesus, each clenching a long metal spike and a heavy wooden mallet in their hands.

Thankfully the soldiers blocked my view so I couldn't see the spikes being driven through Christ's wrists, but I heard the sickening crack of bone and the creak of splintering wood as the swinging hammers found their mark. A moment later one of the soldiers completed the job, spiking Jesus's feet to the cross in the same vicious manner. The ladders were pulled down and the soldiers headed off to crucify the next condemned man listed on the morning duty roster.

There he was: Jesus Christ on the cross. It was an image I had seen in one form or another every day of my life: in the world's greatest works of art, in hand-carved souvenirs sold at shrines by local artists, adorning the necks of friends, in every church I ever entered, marking the site of traffic fatalities, in cemeteries, on ambulances, on the walls of my family's home, on my night table, and even tied onto the machetes the killers used during their evil rampages. And I had one in my hand right now, attached to my father's red-and-white rosary.

The image of Christ's death was ubiquitous in my life, but I never fully understood his suffering until I witnessed it through the rosary. His body told the story of his physical anguish in the language of blood and broken bones, ripped flesh and gaping wounds, and the wheezing rattle of punctured lungs.

But it was his eyes that spoke the story of his psychic and emotional torment. The soft brown eyes he had inherited from his mother studied the faces of those gathering below him now that the last spike had been driven home. His eyes showed no sign of physical pain, but they expressed a sadness so profound there is nothing in my experience to compare it with.

Many of the priests and officials behind the execution were there to mock and gloat over their success. One of them laughed as he taunted: "Look, the man who was going to save us all—he can't even save himself! If you are the Messiah, climb down off your cross right now, and we will believe every word you tell us!"

A group of soldiers crouching on the ground nearby who were rolling dice for Christ's confiscated clothing chuckled at the priest's barb. One shouted out that if the Son of God came down from the cross he'd personally hand him back his clothes, pour him a glass of wine, and climb up onto the cross himself. Then he walked up to Jesus and spat on him. "I didn't think so," he sneered.

Dozens of people laughed and jeered and spat on him. And soon they started to chant, "Son of God—save yourself, come down from your cross. Son of God—save yourself, come down from your cross."

Jesus absorbed the hatred and anger emanating from those who'd come to revel in his suffering and humiliate him further. The deep, deep sadness in his eyes was now offset by the strange expression I'd seen on his face and been so struck by while meditating on the Scourging at the Pillar: the look was one of pity and love. There was no trace of anger or bitterness, no want of vengeance or retribution, no hint of accusation or rancor or reproach. There was only pity and love.

And then Our Lord looked skyward and said the words I had read a thousand times and listened to in a hundred sermons, but until that moment had never fully *heard* before: "Forgive them, Father, they know not what they do."

That simple prayer pierced my soul and lodged in my very being. I wasn't sure exactly what I was feeling, but something shifted within me. It was like the nearly indiscernible seismic tremors that can only occasionally be felt after tectonic plates buckle deep below ground— those slight tremors signal that an awesome power deep within the earth has been released and is about to shake the world. I sensed something like that was about to happen to me, but had no idea what or when.

The howling mob had thinned and others had gathered at the cross, none of whom were taunting Christ. Many of them were the mourning women who had wept for him as he carried his cross along the road to Calvary. The wails had softened to lilting, melancholy moans.

Mary stood in the center of the group, flanked by Mary Magdalene and the apostle John. Her face was drawn and her eyes red after crying so many tears that she had none left. The eyes of mother and son met and for a moment the joy of their past, the pain of their present, and the glory of the future seemed to freeze time itself. In that instant I saw that the prophecy of Simeon—who told Mary in the temple 33 years earlier that her child's suffering would one day pierce her heart like a spear—had been heartbreakingly fulfilled.

Then Jesus said to his sorrowing mother, "Woman, behold thy son." And looking at John, he said, "Behold thy mother."

That moment between grieving mother and dying child seemed too much for the world itself to endure. The sky grew dark and the air so heavy that all sound was stifled into silence. Christ raised his anguished voice to heaven: "My God, my God, why have You forsaken me?" Soon his head began to nod, and he knew that what he had been sent to do had been done. He drew his last breath and formed his last sentence: "Father, into Your hands I commend my spirit."

At this point, two Roman soldiers approached the cross. One fell to his knees trembling, realizing in horror that he had just crucified the Son of God. The other thrust his spear into Jesus's side to check if he was still alive. He watched as blood and water flowed from the wound, and was satisfied Christ was dead.

The sky continued to darken, and the ground shook beneath me. Although it was around noon, the light had all but drained from the day. In shadowy silhouette, I watched Mary kneel at the foot of the cross and cradle the body of her dead boy in her loving arms.

Eᴀᴄʜ Gᴏsᴘᴇʟ ʜᴀs ɪᴛs ᴏᴡɴ rich account of the Crucifixion, and I encourage a thorough reading of all of them to get the most from this mystery. But having said that, I love the account in Mark for what it *doesn't* say. It describes details of the execution of the Son of God as a police report might—with "just the facts" of exact location, precise time, and potential witnesses. For me, it emphasizes how we humans can be blind to the truth, even the greatest truth, and how casually we let God leave our lives without even noticing He was there in the first place. See for yourself in this biblical description:

> Then they brought Jesus to the place called Golgotha (which means the place of a skull). And they offered him wine mixed with myrrh; but he did not take it. And they crucified him, and divided his clothes among them, casting lots to decide what each should take.
>
> It was nine o'clock in the morning when they crucified him (Mark 15:22–25).

Reflecting on this particular mystery while I was hiding was an extremely powerful experience, formed and shaped through many repeated meditations over many weeks. There were days in hiding when I prayed the rosary from the moment I awoke until I passed out with my beads in my hand and prayers on my lips.

To me, the Rosary Mysteries are both a singular and cumulative experience. On the one hand, each time we meditate upon a mystery provides a unique experience bringing its own meaning, message, and reward. On the other hand, all of those single meditations inform and deepen each of our subsequent ones, making our cumulative meditations all the richer and their fruit that much greater. In short, I think the more we pray the rosary and meditate on the stories, the more spiritual wisdom we accumulate.

I mention this now because in this mystery, when I heard Jesus say, "Forgive them, Father, they know not what they do," I really did feel something change in me. That change would take some time to burst into my mind through prayer and open communication with God, but it took root while reflecting on the Fifth Sorrowful Mystery.

The change I am talking about is the central theme of my first book, *Left to Tell*. Once again, I don't want to go too deeply into that book, but suffice it to say that those words of Christ are what helped me let go of the deep anger and hatred I felt toward the killers, anger and hatred that blocked me from giving my heart completely over to God's love. Seeing Jesus forgive his killers and tormentors made me understand that I could do this as well. It would take me a while to get there, but I did. Eventually, I was able to pray the Lord's Prayer in its entirety, not having to skip over the part where we ask God to forgive our trespasses as we forgive those who trespass against us.

I have learned that we can't love when there is hatred in our hearts. What repeated meditations of this mystery helped prepare me to do was to forgive the killers; and once forgiven, my heart no longer had any need to hate them. God's love was able to pour in, and the devil's hold on me through doubt and fear all but vanished.

Forgiveness and love is an ongoing process, and for me that process began while meditating on the Sorrowful Mysteries on the floor of a filthy bathroom while being hunted by killers. And so I prayed:

*Dear God, You have given me so much to be thankful for, and now I have to thank You for a gift that no Father should have to make: the gift of Your own son. You let him come to us because ever since Adam and Eve, You knew we were in trouble and needed Your help, guidance, and love . . . and we did need it, Father, and You know we still do.*

*You loved us so much that You watched Your only son die on the cross for us. I can feel Your sorrow, and I am so sorry You saw him suffer that terribly. And yet You let him come here out of love for us, to show us how to love and treat each other. He is such a good example of what we should all try to be like, and You know we need his example. Look what is happening here in Rwanda—we have forgotten Your love as well as how to love our fellow man, and now we are killing each other out of hatred and fear. But I know Your merciful heart won't give up on us. Thank You for Your love and for Jesus's love.*

*And, God, thank You for our Blessed Mother. Dear Mother Mary, your heart died on the cross with your son . . . I can only imagine what it is like to watch your child in such pain. You have been such a good mother to me. Jesus really meant it when he said you are the mother of all of us. I feel you here in the bathroom with me . . . I feel so close to you. Thank you for teaching me how to love Jesus and to appreciate his sacrifice and truly follow in his footsteps.*

*Please, Mother, watch over those who are suffering so much during this war; and, Mother, let those babies and innocent people being murdered fly into your hands right to heaven. Protect them from desperation—show them your face so they are not scared by the killers. Protect them from the hands of evil. I love you, Mother. Amen.*

# PART V

# THE GLORIOUS MYSTERIES

## (Traditionally Prayed on Wednesdays and Sundays)

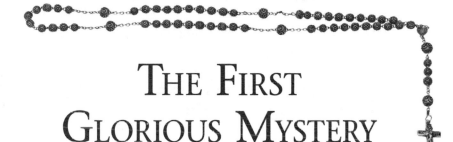

# CHAPTER 21

# THE FIRST GLORIOUS MYSTERY

## The Resurrection

I was probably four years old when I first heard the term *Glorious Mystery*. That's about the time my father invited me to join him and my mother and brothers in evening rosary prayers. Dad always announced which mystery the family would reflect upon on a given evening, and "Glorious" was the first one I remember hearing mentioned.

My excited imagination instantly anticipated hearing a story about the incredibly awesome and amazing powers of God Almighty. Today, more than three decades and countless thousands of rosary meditations later, I still expect the same thing when I start to reflect on a Glorious Mystery—and I am never disappointed. That's because these five mysteries *are* all about the incredibly awesome and amazing powers of God Almighty!

Unlike the Sorrowful Mysteries, where I discovered the depth of God's love for me while reflecting upon Jesus's pain and suffering, the First Glorious Mystery exposed me to the raw and awe-inspiring magnitude of the most

powerful force in the universe: God Himself. These meditations reinforced my faith that my Father, the Creator
of heaven and earth, was capable of doing anything; and
that if I believed in Him enough, He would do anything
for me. That was a comforting thought when I was trapped
in Pastor Murinzi's bathroom and killers were tearing the
house apart looking for me.

My heart felt quite light and carefree when I first
arrived at the Blessed Mother's side after announcing the
First Glorious Mystery. Despite all the love the Sorrowful
Mysteries had brought into my heart, focusing on them
had been emotionally draining to say the least. So I was
looking forward to meditating on mysteries where I could
see Mary crowned Queen of Heaven instead of bearing
witness to Our Lord being flogged.

Once I'd settled into my precious place upon Mary's
lap, the first image to appear in my mind's eye was of
flickering shafts of morning sunlight striking a large, cir-
cular boulder in front of the entrance to a tomb. I knew
immediately that this was where Jesus's shrouded body
had been temporarily put to rest after he was crucified.
A deep, fresh rut in the ground indicated that the heavy
boulder had been recently rolled away from the entrance.

Then I noticed Mary Magdalene standing beside the
boulder, staring into the tomb. She gasped in dismay and
ran off down a well-worn path through the beautiful garden growing in front of the tomb. From my Bible reading,
I knew that because Jesus promised to rise from the dead
three days after his crucifixion, the authorities ordered
his tomb sealed and guards posted at the entrance. They
feared that Christ's followers would steal the body, making it appear that he had risen, thereby proving he really
was the Son of God.

But the soldiers guarding the tomb abandoned their post when an angel appeared at the tomb and rolled the heavy stone away. That's just about the time that Mary Magdalene showed up. She looked into the tomb and saw Our Lord was gone, so she ran sobbing to the apostles Peter and John bewailing the theft of Jesus's body: "They have taken the Lord out of the tomb, and we do not know where they have laid him! (John 20:2)."

A moment later I was in the tomb with Peter and John, who were out of breath from hurrying to get there as fast as they could after hearing Mary Magdalene's story. I watched as the two male disciples, perhaps the closest to Jesus, searched the empty tomb and examined the discarded shroud. They looked at each other in surprise and concluded that if Jesus was gone, he really must be the Son of God. Then they left.

Next I saw Mary Magdalene back at the mouth of the tomb, but this time she was crying. Suddenly a great light shone from the tomb, and she looked inside . . . only to be greeted by two angles who asked why she was weeping. She replied that someone had taken Jesus from her and she didn't know when she would see him again.

At that moment Christ appeared beside the young woman. While he resembled his former self when he was a living man, he also looked quite different somehow, as though he were shrouded in a transparent veil dividing this world from the hereafter. At first she didn't recognize him— but when she heard her beloved Lord speak her name, she knew that he had risen and was standing before her.

Mary Magdalene reached out to Jesus, but he stopped her: "Do not touch me, for I am not yet ascended to my Father." He told her to go tell the others that he had risen from the dead and that she had seen him herself. He promised that he would see them all soon, before he went to join the Father in heaven. And then he was gone.

THE ACCOUNTS OF THE RESURRECTION in the four Gospels are all similar and yet quite different—even contradictory—at the same time, so I encourage everyone to read as much from all of them as possible when preparing to reflect on this mystery. Here are a few places to start: Matthew 27:57–28:9, Mark 16:1–11, Luke 24:1–12, and John 19:40–20:18. Please don't feel overwhelmed—read one at a time and enjoy, as they are all wonderful!

The passage I draw on the most for inspiration is when the risen Jesus calls to the weeping Mary Magdalene by name:

> Jesus said to her, "Mary!" She turned and said to him in Hebrew, "Rabbouni!" (which means Teacher). Jesus said to her, "Do not hold on to me, because I have not yet ascended to the Father. But go to my brothers and say to them, 'I am ascending to my Father and your Father, to my God and your God.'" Mary Magdalene went and announced to the disciples, "I have seen the Lord"; and she told them that he had said these things to her (John 20:16–18).

As I reflected on this mystery I was struck by how important it was as it pertained to absolutely everyone and everything connected to our religion.

At a very personal level, I realized that, yes, God has the power to do anything. And if we have faith, that power can belong to us, His children. Also, the Resurrection showed me that when God makes a promise, He is going to keep it. The amount of hope that simple realization gave me was immeasurable.

Passages from the Bible containing the Lord's promises to us flooded through my mind, and I scoured my Good Book looking for more. There were so many, from the encouraging ones that we use in everyday speech (such as "knock and the door will be opened unto thee," or "seek and ye shall find") to the more essential promises of salvation, such as those found in John 14:6, when Jesus promises us that "I am the way, and the truth, and the life. No one comes to the Father except through me."

What I found most personally empowering, and that seemed to encapsulate all the promises, came from Matthew 17:20: "For truly I tell you, if you have faith the size of a mustard seed, you will say to this mountain, 'Move from here to there,' and it will move; and nothing will be impossible for you." While I was in the bathroom, that promise became part of my inner self, and I prayed for the faith and trust to believe it completely and without doubt. It gave me the courage to start studying English in the bathroom, so I'd be prepared to start a new life when the killing ended—which I did with some success.

The only reason I achieved this was because I believed the promises God made to us . . . and the greatest promise ever made, and ever kept, was the Resurrection of Christ.

When I meditated more deeply I saw that the fulfilled promise of the Resurrection was the cornerstone of Christianity. If it had not happened, there would be no Catholic Church; I would never have learned to pray the rosary; and, in all likelihood, I would have been murdered by machete or spear on the pastor's bathroom floor. Jesus promised he would rise from the dead. If he had not risen, his promise would have meant nothing—worse than nothing, it would have been a lie. And Christianity would not have survived if it was founded on a lie. As the Apostle Paul said while discussing the Resurrection with fledgling Christians: "If Christ has not been raised, your faith is futile (1 Corinthians 15:17)."

Perhaps the greatest and most glorious promise of all revealed in the Resurrection is the promise of a life after death—and not only is it an eternal life, but one we get to spend eternally with Jesus.

ONE OF THE MOST IMPORTANT LESSONS I learned while meditating upon this mystery is that because God keeps His promises to us, we must likewise keep our promises to Him—following His commandments and living as He has directed us to live.

This is a lesson I have reminded myself each day since leaving the bathroom and one I will continue to remind myself for all the days I have remaining. And so I prayed:

> *Dear God, thank You for always keeping Your promises to us, even if we don't always believe that You will. Every day I feel more certain that You will deliver me from the hell that we are living. I know that, if it is Your will, you will raise me from the stench of death that is all around us here, into a new life where I promise that I will serve You always.*
>
> *Please keep filling my heart with faith . . . even Peter and John had not fully believed that Jesus was Your son until they found his tomb was empty. So, if such great disciples had doubts . . . maybe You will forgive me when I have my own, and help me grow in faith each day.*
>
> *Please look after my family wherever they are. Amen.*

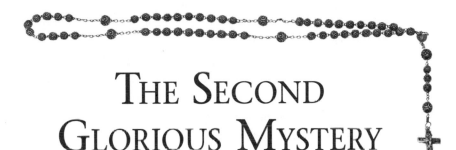

# CHAPTER 22

# THE SECOND GLORIOUS MYSTERY

## The Ascension

When I was 12 years old and preparing for my rosary test, I remember how surprised I was by the story associated with the Second Glorious Mystery. I guess up until then I had just assumed that after Jesus died, he was resurrected on the third day, made several appearances to his apostles and followers, and went up to heaven. But then I read a few stories about what the apostles did after Jesus was crucified, and I had to smack myself in the forehead and say, "Wow, was I ever wrong!"

I discovered that after his resurrection Jesus spent 40 days traveling through the Holy Land, appearing to all manner of people before ascending into heaven. This gave me much to meditate upon after reciting my opening prayers and announcing that I was about to reflect upon the Ascension.

The Blessed Mother and I were sitting together in a garden watching Jesus greet several people beside his tomb, including Mary herself. She was looking much older thanks to the strain of enduring his ordeal, but still beaming with joy as she looked at her risen son. Our Lord moved easily, as though his battered body had been mended in death; however, the wounds at the base of his hands and on his feet looked as fresh as if the spikes had been driven through them that morning.

The scene quickly shifted to evening, and there was Christ sitting at a table, having dinner with several men and women I did not recognize. He ate and drank with them and seemed to be instructing them on how to spread the message of his word.

A moment later I saw Jesus and the Apostle Thomas standing in the center of a room. Until that moment Thomas had not seen the risen Messiah and refused to believe the others who swore they had talked with him personally. Jesus presented Thomas with his upturned hands and the spear wound on his side, so that the doubting disciple could put his fingers into the wounds to bolster his faith. Thomas stepped back, aghast at the suggestion, and deeply ashamed that he had ever doubted the Lord had resurrected as he'd promised.

Christ blessed Thomas for his belief, and suddenly he was outside and walking along the shores of the Sea of Galilee, speaking to a half dozen of his disciples. And then once again he moved, this time to a hillside where he passed among a crowd of 400 or 500 people, talking freely to all who approached him.

Next I saw Jesus walking through the same grove of olive trees I had seen him in the night before his crucifixion —which meant he was on Mount Olivet, and 40 days had passed since he died.

As Jesus slowly made his way up the long slope, the remaining apostles began falling in alongside him. Together they walked to the top of the steep hill, from where they could see Jerusalem spreading out before them far below. The gold and bronze that decorated the marble pillars of the city's towering temple reflected the sunlight that shimmered and pulsed like a burning heart.

Christ pointed to the city, then turned to his disciples and told them not to leave Jerusalem. It was there, he said, that he would send the Holy Spirit to baptize them all in just a matter of days. He told them that the moment the Spirit was upon them, they would be filled with the power to convert the hearts of men and spread the word of Christ to every corner of the earth.

Jesus then opened his arms wide as though to embrace the world, and drifted upward toward heaven upon a silver cloud. The apostles watched in amazement as Christ ascended higher and higher until he was encircled in a brilliant pool of white light and vanished from sight beyond the gates of heaven—where, at long last, he took his rightful seat on the right-hand side of his Father.

The apostles continued to stare skyward in wonder, until angels appeared beside them disguised as men but wearing shining white cloaks. The angels snapped the apostles out of their trance by asking them why they continued to look toward heaven, when Jesus had told them he would soon return to them.

The apostles looked at each other and realized the angels were right. So, with their faces aglow with happiness and hope, they made their way down from Mount Olivet and toward Jerusalem, where Our Lord had told them to wait for the Holy Spirit to come upon them.

THE FULLEST ACCOUNT OF THE ASCENSION in the Bible is as follows:

---

After his suffering he presented himself alive to them by many convincing proofs, appearing to them during forty days and speaking about the kingdom of God. While staying with them, he ordered them not to leave Jerusalem, but to wait there for the promise of the Father. "This," he said, "is what you have heard from me; for John baptized with water, but you will be baptized with the Holy Spirit not many days from now."

So when they had come together, they asked him, "Lord, is this the time when you will restore the kingdom to Israel?" He replied, "It is not for you to know the times or periods that the Father has set by his own authority. But you will receive power when the Holy Spirit has come upon you; and you will be my witnesses in Jerusalem, in all Judea and Samaria, and to the ends of the earth." When he had said this, as they were watching, he was lifted up, and a cloud took him out of their sight. While he was going and they were gazing up towards heaven, suddenly two men in white robes stood by them. They said, "Men of Galilee, why do you stand looking up toward heaven? This Jesus, who has been taken up from you into heaven, will come in the same way as you saw him go into heaven" (Acts 1:3–11).

---

As I reflected on the Ascension Mystery, I was moved by the love Jesus continued to exhibit to everyone he encountered. Even though he had been betrayed and denied by the people dearest to him, and beaten and tortured by those he had come to save, he was the same after his horrific experiences as he had been before: gentle, loving, patient, and kind.

He chose to remain here among us for 40 more days, when he could have been in Paradise with his loving Father and the entire celestial host singing his praises. He knew the disciples still had much to learn from him. He wanted to make sure that before they set off on their ministries they knew how to plant the seeds of love and forgiveness in the hearts of men, so that one day the Word of God would be spoken in every language and alive in every heart.

THE FACT THAT OUR LORD didn't speak one word about the horrible things that had been done to him made me believe that, no matter how much my own sins may offend him, Jesus will always love and forgive me. Seeing him in this mystery had, as it did with Thomas, strengthened my faith and filled my heart with hope that Jesus was waiting for me patiently and all would be forgiven. So I prayed:

> *Dear God, thank You for letting Jesus stay with us after we had treated him so terribly. I'm sure it pained You to see him beaten, hurt, and brutalized by killers. I know how You feel when I think of what may be happening to my parents or brothers right now, even as I am talking to You. If they came to me and told me they had been beaten and tortured by our neighbors but insisted on going back to help them mend their ways, I would call them crazy, wrap my arms around them, and never let them go. But You let Jesus come*

*back to us; and because of that, people everywhere know that his love and redemption are there for anyone who reaches out to him. I pray that when You deliver me from this bathroom, I will be as kind and forgiving to the killers I meet as Jesus was to everyone he encountered.*

*Please look out for my family wherever they are . . . talking to You about them like this has made my heart ache. Please, can I give that pain to You like You tell us we can in the Bible? Thank You, it's all Yours. Amen.*

# CHAPTER 23

# THE THIRD GLORIOUS MYSTERY

## The Descent of the Holy Spirit

While I was in hiding, I often called upon the power of the Holy Spirit to cover me like a magnificent, impenetrable shield that would conceal and protect me if or when the killers kicked in Pastor Murinzi's bathroom door with their machetes raised high and ready to swing.

When I was much younger, I used to pester Father Clement, my favorite and most knowledgeable parish priest, for an explanation of how the Holy Trinity worked. From reading my catechism handbooks I understood that the Trinity was made up of three equal entities: Father, Son, and Holy Spirit. And I was very confident in my knowledge of God and Jesus, but what was the Holy Spirit exactly and what did it do?

Father Clement told me that brilliant theologians had been asking and arguing over that same question for centuries. And then he offered me his own learned opinion, which I have held in my heart and mind ever since. "Immaculée, think of the Holy Spirit as God's love moving within us, and remember that God's love is the most powerful force in the universe," he explained. "The Holy Spirit fills us with grace and shows us the truth when we receive Christ into our hearts. It enlightens us and empowers us with an understanding of the Word of God— the Spirit directs us, teaches us, guides us, and strengthens us through faith." I've always remembered the priest's brief but ever so beautiful definition of the Holy Spirit: *God's love moving within us.*

It was with that definition in my heart that I began reciting the opening prayers of the Third Glorious Mystery. Moments later I was delivered to my peaceful place of meditation, in the lap of the Blessed Mother. Then, before I knew it, I was back in the same room where Jesus had shared the Last Supper with his 12 apostles on the eve of the Crucifixion. It was 10 days after Christ had ascended to heaven; 50 days since he had risen from the dead.

Gathered around the familiar wooden table were 11 of the original apostles, as well as a newcomer—a man called Matthias, who had been chosen to replace Judas since Judas had hung himself after betraying the Lord. Farther back in the room I saw Mary moving in and out of the flickering light cast by the lamps upon the apostles' table. Her face, as it had been so often when I looked upon it in meditation, was radiant and serene. She was talking gently, but I couldn't see whom she was addressing. I did sense that many of Jesus's followers were sitting in the shadows, waiting with the apostles for him to fulfill the promise he had made to them atop Mount Olivet: to send the Holy Spirit to baptize them.

As I watched the apostles eat and chat with each other, I became aware of a buzzing in my ears, as though a mosquito had just flown into the room. Then the dishes on the apostles' table began rattling against each other and falling onto the floor, and soon the entire room began to shake. The soft drone grew louder and louder until I feared I would be deafened. I clapped my hands over my ears for protection, but the sound only increased in my mind, no matter how hard I plugged my ears.

It reminded me of the time I was taken to Kigali International Airport to see my first jet airplane, and stood on the edge of the airfield looking up as the massive plane roared by just above my head. It was the loudest noise I had ever heard, but that was a whisper compared to what I was experiencing at this moment.

Suddenly a brilliant white light, the same one that had enveloped Jesus when he ascended to heaven, cast the apostles' faces with a luster that washed away all the pain and sorrow stamped upon them through the trauma they suffered during Our Lord's last days. Then the light increased until it was nearly blinding, as 12 burning tongues of fire appeared above each apostle's head. The very air seemed aflame in searing red, orange, and gold.

Everything and everyone in the room seemed to be frozen in time and space, and the only motion was found in the shimmering pool of light encircling the apostles. The flames flared higher and then descended toward their heads, until the fire seemed to pass through the top of their skulls and disappear. I watched in wonder as the flames reappeared in their eyes . . . which now burned with the passion, wisdom, and love of Christ.

The unearthly roaring ended as suddenly as it had begun, and the apostles stood up, appearing as though they had grown in strength and stature. They looked like giants among men. They faced each other and began sharing the messages of Our Lord in an excited, chaotic burst of inspired communication composed of every language of the ancient world.

The room then vanished from my sight, and my mind was filled with a rapid succession of shifting images in which I saw the apostles—sometimes alone, sometimes in groups—baptizing those who had come to them hungering for Christ, and preaching to vast crowds in locations reflecting every imaginable place on Earth, from mountainside meadows to forested valleys, from desert plains to the salt-sprayed decks of ships at sea.

THE MOST DETAILED BIBLICAL ACCOUNT of the Third Glorious Mystery is this one:

When the day of Pentecost had come, they were all together in one place. And suddenly from heaven there came a sound like the rush of a violent wind, and it filled the entire house where they were sitting. Divided tongues, as of fire, appeared among them, and a tongue rested on each of them. All of them were filled with the Holy Spirit and began to speak in other languages, as the Spirit gave them ability (Acts 2:1–4).

While reflecting on this miraculous mystery, I gradually understood that watching the Holy Spirit descend upon the apostles was in a way like witnessing the birth of the Church and of Christianity itself. It was the Holy Spirit that endowed the 12 men with the wisdom, passion, faith, and courage to speak what Christ spoke and to inspire the hearts of men to seek God. It was the Holy Spirit that gave the apostles the courage to travel to the ends of civilization to spread God's word and the messages of Christ, to be willing to die in Jesus's name, and to become martyrs of the faith. And it was the power of the Holy Spirit that enabled the apostles to cast out demons and work miracles.

MEDITATING UPON THE HOLY SPIRIT'S incredible power helped me realize that as long as my faith was strong, the love of God would indeed move within me and nothing was beyond my reach. That knowledge bolstered my faith that, not only would I escape the bathroom, but the Holy Spirit would direct me after the genocide in a life dedicated to sharing and spreading God's message of love and forgiveness. My faith was rewarded. Today, whenever I prepare to speak to a group of people or sit down to write something I intend to share with others, I invite the Holy Spirit into my heart to help inspire and guide me.

And so I prayed:

> *Dear God, thank You for sending the Holy Spirit to inspire the apostles to carry Your message of love and forgiveness across the world. The gifts the Holy Spirit gave the apostles were so, so powerful . . . otherwise, there would be no Christianity here today, 2,000 years later.*
>
> *So please, send the Holy Spirit to protect me now, to blind the killers when they come into the house looking for me and these other ladies—who are even more frightened than I am, if that is possible. Even better would be for the Holy Spirit to enter the hardened hearts of all the killers in this country and make them drop their machetes and stop hurting us . . . but I know You have your plan, God, and that plan is a mystery to us. But I promise You that if it is part of Your plan for me to live through this nightmare, I will invite the Holy Spirit into my heart every day and ask*

*to be as inspired as the apostles were when they trav-
eled around the world telling everyone about Your love
and forgiveness.*

*Please watch out for my family, and if anything
bad has happened to them, keep them safe in heaven
with You until I get there to see them again. Amen.*

# CHAPTER 24

# THE FOURTH GLORIOUS MYSTERY

## The Assumption

The last two Glorious Mysteries are unique among all the mysteries because the events they describe are not recorded in any biblical passage, but are based on belief, theology, and Catholic tradition stretching all the way back to the apostolic age. So while they may not be found in the New Testament, they don't contradict any scriptural teachings and actually support and enhance our understanding of these stories in a manner that is both heartwarming and beautiful. And, as you are about to see, the Fourth and Fifth Glorious Mysteries have a special meaning for me personally because they focus on my favorite and most beloved of all the saints, my dear Heavenly Mother, the Virgin Mary.

While I was in hiding, meditating upon the Fourth Glorious Mystery was a surefire way to ease the anxiety brought on by my own trials and tribulations. You see, the Assumption describes the event in which Mary, after enduring more suffering and sadness than any mother, was rewarded in the sweetest and most tender way imaginable.

As always, I found myself in the company of the Blessed Mother as soon as I had completed my opening prayers and had announced my intention to meditate upon the Assumption. It was such a happy meditation for me because I was able to reflect upon the life of Mary and the incredible and critical role she played both in the history of the world and the history of our salvation.

The first image I beheld was that of the fresh-faced teenaged girl whose flawless skin radiated with a glowing health and beauty so perfect it seemed otherworldly. And then I saw an even more impossibly beautiful Mary, carrying Jesus in her womb, during her visit to her cousin Elizabeth, who was also pregnant. Both women were filled with the Holy Spirit, Mary's voice rising to the heavens singing the Magnificat in glorification of God.

Next I was with the Blessed Mother in the humble manger, the baby Jesus in a bed of hay at her side. Despite the squalor of their lowly circumstances, she emanated a maternal love that would one day light the world. Then my mind took me from the manger to a road between Nazareth and Jerusalem, and to the tortured days she and Joseph spent searching for the lost child—a suffering that ended in a happy reunion at the temple.

In seconds, I advanced decades and was celebrating at the wedding in Cana, where I witnessed Mary firmly requesting that her dutiful boy miraculously produce wine where there was none. In doing so she initiated Christ's first miracle and set him on his mission to save humankind. Then I watched with sadness as she witnessed the betrayal, the trial, and the torture of her son as she followed Jesus on his long agonizing journey to the cross. My heart melted as she stood looking up at him as he was about to surrender his spirit to God, but ignored his pain long enough to place her in the care of John, his most beloved disciple.

I saw her weeping over her son's dead body as she cradled him in her arms atop Cavalry; then at his tomb, where her face was lit up with joy upon seeing Jesus risen from the dead.

And then, in a series of images, I beheld Mary's life after Jesus's spirit had departed this world. I saw her being cared for by, and caring for, John, but she also traveled to visit and tend to the needs of the other apostles engaged in the mission of spreading the word of God far and wide. She offered them counsel and comfort, tended their wounds and helped them teach, fed them meals and nourished their spirits, reminding them always by her presence and through her immaculate heart of the love of Our Lord.

At last, slowed by age, but diminished in neither her beauty nor her faith, she grew weary and took to her bed to rest. Those who remained of the original apostles knelt at her side to offer her comfort and bid her farewell, as did many new and faithful disciples of Christ.

There was no heaviness upon my heart as I watched the Blessed Mother close her eyes and slip gently into the sleep of death, for as she left this life after years of faithful service to God, a smile appeared on her peaceful face. She had gone to join her only child.

Still, those beside her sobbed silently at parting company with the handmaiden of the Lord; the young virgin who had given birth to baby Jesus and reared and nurtured him so well; the mother who raised the boy into the man they called Christ the Savior; the mature woman who was the most beloved servant of God, who was a mother to them all, and who was now the Mother of the World.

I watched as many holy women lovingly prepared her body for the burial, and as the apostles carried her from the house to a nearby garden tomb where they laid her to rest. The next image that presented itself to my mind was that of the apostles and hundreds of Christ's new followers arriving early the next morning at Mary's tomb to pray as the sun began to rise. But the tomb was empty, filled only with the fragrant scent of wild roses and jasmine and echoing with the sweet sound of countless songbirds.

Jesus would not allow corruption to touch his mother, who had been conceived and born without the stain of sin, and who lived and left her life with no blemish upon her soul. Instead, he came to fetch her home himself. He carried her body and soul into paradise intact, instructing the heavenly host to prepare for her a place of honor.

AS I MENTIONED, THE STORY OF Mary's Assumption was not recorded in the scriptures, but was well known and shared by early Christians and has been part of Catholic tradition for most of its 2,000-year history. In 1950 Pope Pius XII declared the Assumption of Mary as official Church doctrine:

By the authority of our Lord Jesus Christ, of the Blessed Apostles Peter and Paul, and by our own authority, we pronounce, declare, and define it to be a divinely revealed dogma: that the Immaculate Mother of God, the ever Virgin Mary, having completed the course of her earthly life, was assumed body and soul into heavenly glory (Pope Pius XII, *Munificentissimus Deus*, 44).

Reflecting upon this mystery while in hiding was a continual source of comfort and joy for me. I had always regarded the Blessed Mother as my mom in heaven and had reserved a special place in my heart for her before the genocide. But, as you have surely gleaned from the pages of this book, during the genocide the Virgin Mary became my truest guardian angel; my most steadfast companion; my counselor, consoler, and comforter. She guided me through the mysteries and, regardless of how painful they were for her or for me, she made me focus on the love, suffering, and words of Christ and draw their meaning and messages deep into the well of my heart—a constant source of solace, truth, and peace. She did not fight my battles against the devil for me, but taught me how to fight on my own—with her rosary, the love of her son, and a faith in God, which she fostered until it flourished.

THE PRAYERS OF THE ROSARY BROUGHT ME to the Blessed Mother each and every day during the genocide, and she never left my side, nor I hers.

Watching her die with the grace of a happy death when so many around me were dying by the devil's hand gave me hope that when my time came, I would meet death with the same smile I beheld upon the beautiful, radiant face of my heavenly mother and dearest friend, the Virgin Mary. And so I prayed:

*Dear God, for months the Blessed Mother has sat by my side and encouraged me to seek You out, to listen to Your words with my heart instead of my ears. She has guided me to You, and You have lifted me up in Your arms and showed me how to love and forgive. I do not know if I shall live another day or die before this hour has passed. But I do know that You love me, as You loved Mary . . . and if it is Your will I die, please teach me how to say good-bye to this life that I cling to so fiercely with the same courage and grace of your beloved handmaiden, Mary.*

*And please, God, watch over my mother on Earth—her lungs are weak, and she is not as strong as Mary and needs your help. Also, remember my prayers for my dad and brothers. Amen.*

# CHAPTER 25

# THE FIFTH GLORIOUS MYSTERY

## The Coronation of Mary as Queen of Heaven

The fifth and final Glorious Mystery, like the Assumption of Mary, is an event that is not recorded in scripture but dates back in Christian tradition, devotion, and sacred theology to the days when the religion was just beginning to spread beyond the Holy Land along the shores of the Mediterranean Sea. References to Mary as the Queen of Heaven can be found in ancient texts tracing back to as early as the 4th century; and, presumably, the title was upon the lips of the faithful long before that.

Meditating upon the Fifth Glorious Mystery when I was hiding in the bathroom gave me a much-needed sense of empowerment—for I knew that Mary, my companion and confidante, was regarded so highly by the Creator of the universe that she was crowned Queen of Heaven. It was comforting to know that a woman whom I called my friend had been granted such a title, status, and honor by such infinitely powerful beings.

When I had finished my opening prayers and was sitting with my head in the Blessed Mother's lap, I was struck by how her presence in these moments always felt the same to me: comforting, protective, instructive, caring, kind, and above all, loving. But never, not once, did I feel she was proudly regal or had ever felt personally elevated by the pomp of royalty. She was first and foremost my Mother, and luckily for me, I was her grateful daughter. When Mary was with me in the bathroom, the devil hid his face and shut his lying mouth in fear—and every saint and angel in heaven bowed to her majesty and called her "My Lady" and "Your Highness."

Unlike most of my meditations, this one was more intuitive than visual, as though I were watching the event play out behind multiple layers of fine gossamer. My sense was that Mary was seated on a high throne wearing a dress of flowing purple, her beautiful and dark flowing hair covered in the sheerest lace veil. A long line of archangels, angels, cherubs, and saints flanked her throne, forming a corridor between them that stretched out into infinity. Voices too sweet to be described sang Our Lady's praises in words that were captured and carried to the stars by the strains of heavenly harps and the muffled blasts of countless horns—horns that soon announced the arrival of the Lord.

From far off in the distance, three gleaming pillars of intensely burning light floated toward Mary's throne along the corridor created by the attending celestial court.

Mary stood, opened her arms in welcome, and in the passionate voice of the young expectant mom I saw standing before Elizabeth so long ago, she began to sing the Magnificat: "My soul magnifies the Lord, and my spirit rejoices in God my Savior, for he has looked with favor on the lowliness of his servant. Surely, from now on all generations will call me blessed; for the Mighty One has done great things for me, and holy is his name."

The pillars of light increased in brilliance and intensity as they approached Mary, and I knew they must be the Holy Trinity. Mary knelt as Jesus emerged from the light, holding a gleaming bejeweled crown in his outstretched arms, which he gently lowered upon his beloved mother's head. A great cry of joy rose up from heaven that I was certain was loud enough to wake the dead.

AGAIN, THERE ARE NO SCRIPTURAL ACCOUNTS of Mary's Coronation, but Pope Pius XII recognized this glorious event in 1954. At that time, he added the feast of the Queenship of Mary to the official church calendar, which is celebrated every August 22, a week after the Feast of the Assumption:

From the ancient Christian documents, from prayers of the liturgy, from the innate piety of the Christian people, from works of art, from every side we have gathered witnesses to the regal dignity of the Virgin Mother of God; we have likewise shown that the arguments deduced by Sacred Theology from the treasure store of the faith fully confirm this truth. Such a wealth of witnesses makes up a resounding chorus which changes the sublimity of the royal dignity of the Mother of God and of men, to whom every creature is subject, who is "exalted to the heavenly throne, above the choirs of angels" (Pope Pius XII, *Ad Caeli Reginam*, 46).

For me, the Fifth Glorious Mystery is literally the crowning glory of the prayers that brought me to Mary. Of course, the coronation I just described was purely of my imagination, woven and stitched together from what I have read, heard, and dreamed about heaven and this glorious event over the course of my life. And, as in all my meditations and reflections, the images and meanings change with every rosary I recite.

It is the great and enduring beauty of the rosary that its regimented prayers and reflections are wondrously unique and open for individual interpretation and personal growth. At the height of the genocide, when I was at my weakest and most in need, those prayers and meditations opened my closed, terrified, and doubting heart just enough for Mary to find her way in and lead me all the way to Jesus.

MEDITATING ON THE LIFE OF CHRIST as found in the Rosary Mysteries gave me the strength to hold on to my faith during the darkest days I have ever experienced. But far more than that, these prayers and meditations I had learned as a girl and loved since childhood provided the bridge I needed to walk away from the life-destroying, heart-withering, faith-poisoning hatred and anger that threatened to consume me when I finally left the bathroom.

That is when I discovered that, with the exception of my brother Aimable (who had been studying abroad), all of my family had been murdered, along with a million other Tutsis.

Through the prayers and reflections I devoted myself to using my father's red-and-white rosary, I was able to open my heart to God and fill it with His love, and with that love I was able to forgive those who murdered my parents and brothers. In that act of forgiveness, I shook off the devil's voice forever and found the courage and strength to move forward with my life—free from bitterness and anger. And I was able to fulfill the promise I had made to God while cowering on the bathroom floor: to spread His word of love and forgiveness for the rest of my days.

I owe all that to the rosary, the prayer that saved my life. It was a gift to us all from the Queen of Heaven herself, and it is a gift that can save and enrich all our lives . . . and save each of our souls. What greater gift could anyone ever desire?

And so I prayed:

*Thank You, God, for bringing me through the slaughter and teaching me how to replace the hatred and anger that used to fill my heart with love and forgiveness. Thank you, dear Blessed Mother, for loving us all as you loved your son, and for giving St. Dominic the rosary so long ago. Your precious gift has helped so many lost and frightened souls like me find Jesus and hold on to God's love—even in the bleakest hours of our life when it is so easy to surrender to the darkness of despair that the devil uses to entrap our spirits.*

*And, God, I want to thank You as well for the gift of the rosary. When I pray it, I know You love me, and I know You know that I love You. I will always keep my promises to You because I know You will always keep Your promises to me. You are my Father and I am Your servant . . . keep me safe and strong and faithful, especially when I trip and falter the way I often do. Fill me with the Holy Spirit, to guide and help my heart speak truthfully as I endeavor to spread the messages of Christ's love and salvation in Your name. Thy will be done, not mine.*

*And please, look after my mom and dad and my brothers Vianney and Damascene until I get there . . . they always worry about me, but as long as You and Jesus and Mary are with me, You can let them know I am going to be just fine. Amen.*

HERE WOULD BE A FITTING PLACE to share with you the concluding prayer of every rosary I pray, the Hail Holy Queen Prayer:

*Hail Holy Queen, Mother of Mercy, our life, our sweetness, and our hope. To thee do we cry, poor banished children of Eve. To thee do we send up our sighs, mourning and weeping in this valley of tears. Turn, then, most gracious advocate, thine eyes of mercy toward us, and after this, our exile, show unto us the blessed fruit of thy womb, Jesus. O clement, O loving, O sweet Virgin Mary! Amen.*

# EPILOGUE

## *Everyday Miracles*

When I finally walked out of Pastor Murinzi's house 91 days after arriving on his doorstep pleading for help, the Blessed Mother was at my side, just as she had been throughout the genocide. Without her comfort, the death and devastation I encountered would have been unbearable.

During the three dreadful months of the Rwandan holocaust, everything I had ever known had been destroyed or forever changed: my world, my country, myself . . . everything. But the most profound change of all —and what I now consider the first true rosary miracle in my life—was the change in my heart. When I entered the bathroom, my heart was filled with a bitter anger and hatred so deep it threatened to eclipse whatever goodness my soul had once possessed.

Despite the horror I witnessed, my rosary prayers miraculously healed my shattered spirit and guided me safely through the aftermath of the genocide with my faith intact, and with God in my heart. And from the moment I left the bathroom, the miracles never stopped enhancing my life and the lives of so many others I know!

The first miracle occurred within days of saying farewell to Pastor Murinzi, as a group of other Tutsi survivors I was with was being transported by French soldiers to a "safe zone." When distant gunfire startled our protectors, they became afraid and dropped us into the middle of a group of armed Hutu killers.

Some of these men knew my family and had been hunting me for months; they surrounded me, saying how happy they were to finally be able to finish me off. When one of them came at me with his machete, I clutched my rosary and stared into his eyes, offering him all the love in my heart. I recalled the love I had seen in Jesus's eyes when he looked at the angry mobs who ridiculed him, or at the soldiers who nailed him to the cross.

Miraculously, the hardened heart of this Hutu killer was softened by my loving look, and he dropped his machete and walked away in shame. His companions continued to swing their blades in the air and threatened to kill me—but I continued to pray and they backed off, their anger and hatred fading away.

Several weeks after that, I was living in the devastated capital city of Kigali and was on the brink of starvation. Most Tutsi survivors were being herded into overcrowded displaced-persons camps, where Hutu killers were hiding out and where rape and murder were commonplace. The Rwandan economy had collapsed completely, and theft and prostitution were the principal means of support. Yet, through praying my rosary, I managed to find a job where no job existed—at the United Nations.

While in hiding I decided I should learn English (I am certain the Blessed Mother put it into my head) in order to get a job at the UN after the genocide. But the guard at the security gate turned me away time and time again because the UN wasn't hiring—especially not Rwandans. Despite the constant rejection, I persevered: I prayed every night with my father's red-and-white beads and arrived at the UN every morning with renewed faith I'd find a job. Finally, the miracle happened.

One morning the guard just waved me through, and I went to the employment office. Even though I was sent packing from that office because I had no qualifications whatsoever, the Blessed Mother steered me toward a back stairwell . . . where I literally bumped into a man who mistook me for a Tutsi woman he was good friends with before the genocide, and whom he believed to be dead. His heart opened up to me and to my plight, and he assured me he would find me work, which he did! Not only that, through him I found both a career and a mentor who protected me throughout the years I worked at the UN in Rwanda—all thanks to my daily (or nightly!) rosary prayers.

And miracles, both large and small, have continued to bless my life since arriving in America in 1998. I found a great job at the United Nations in Manhattan through praying the rosary and, miracle of miracles, my first book was published after weeks of intensive rosary prayers!

If you remember, when I was in hiding, I promised God that if I survived the genocide I would dedicate my life to spreading His message of love and forgiveness. What better way to spread that message, I reasoned, than by sharing the story of how I found Him during the genocide in a book?

With God's help (and Mary sitting beside me!) I managed to write a manuscript, but had no idea how to get it published. So I took out my rosary and did what I do whenever I need help to accomplish the impossible: I prayed the beads. Within a couple of days I met the incredibly talented inspirational writer and speaker Dr. Wayne Dyer, who told me the world needed to hear my story, and arranged for my book *Left to Tell* to be published.

Thank you, as always, Blessed Mother (and thank you, dear Wayne)! I have now written five books—all of them penned with the rosary (and a good dictionary) in my hand or at my side.

BECAUSE OF THE BOOKS I'VE WRITTEN, I have been invited to speak to people all over the world about how the power of love and forgiveness can transform our hearts and our lives. During my travels I've been blessed with the opportunity to hear many personal stories about rosary miracles from people of incredibly diverse backgrounds and from all walks of life. Here are just a few that I hope will inspire you as much as they have inspired me:

— I met a woman in Poland who was diagnosed with terminal cancer and underwent several years of treatment, and had been given just two more months to live. But her faith was strong; she and her husband locked themselves away for an entire weekend and prayed the rosary around the clock, asking for a cure. When they arrived for a checkup that Monday morning, her doctors could find no trace of the cancer—it had completely vanished!

— In Detroit, I met a young woman who told me that as a college student, her poor grades and desperate financial status threw her into such a debilitating depression she had no option but to drop out of school. But as she was heading to the dean's office to file her formal withdrawal forms, someone gave her one of my books. After reading what the rosary had done for me, she decided to pray with the beads every day for a month . . . and within two weeks her depression had completely lifted, her finances improved, she returned to her classes, and today is a university graduate at the outset of a brilliant career.

— A Protestant man I met in Canada told me his work had caused him so much stress that he began drinking heavily and was on the verge of losing everything—his job, his marriage, and his health. After hearing me talk about the rosary, he decided to try out the "Catholic" beads, and began praying the rosary faithfully with an open heart each morning upon waking. Soon he had lost all desire to drink; he found that his work, which had seemed so stressful, was suddenly exciting and rewarding; and he was happier than ever in his marriage.

— Another man I met in New York told me he had suffered a sudden and unexpected financial loss of many thousands of dollars and was unable to pay his rent. He prayed the rosary that night asking Mary to intercede on his behalf, and the very next morning he was offered a work contract for the exact same sum of money (to the penny!) that he had lost the day before.

— While traveling to the shrine of Our Lady of Lourdes in France, I met a woman who told me that several doctors from different hospitals had told her daughter that she was physically incapable of ever having children. Well, two months after visiting the shrine of Our Lady of Kibeho in Rwanda, where she prayed the rosary asking the Blessed Mother to help her conceive, the young woman became pregnant with twins!

— And then there is a woman I know in Belgium who called me one night in tears. Her brother was about to go in front of an immigration judge who'd been out to get him for years, denying every appeal for permanent residency he'd ever filed. The next morning she and her brother were attending his last appeal hearing, and it was to be in front of the same acrimonious judge.

"I am a Protestant, Immaculée, and I don't go in for the rosary," she said, "but it has done so much for you that I went out and bought one today. Please teach me how to use it!" I stayed on the phone with the woman all night long praying the rosary with her. We prayed until she left with her brother to appear at the hearing.

That evening she called to tell me that she'd never witnessed a more dramatic change of heart in a person than what she'd seen occur that day with the immigration judge. "He went from hating my brother to practically embracing him! He issued him a permanent residency card and wished him the best of luck in his new home-land," she said, through tears of joy.

That was five years ago, and both the woman and her brother, while still faithful Protestants, continue to pray the rosary regularly and swear it continues to bring blessings into their daily lives.

THERE IS ONE LAST STORY I WOULD LIKE to share with you that illustrates the incredible power of the rosary prayers.

A very successful friend of mine who works in the pharmaceutical industry called me one day out of the blue. "We were testing a major new cancer drug and something came up that made me think of you," she said, in a voice that let me know she was smiling as she told me her news. She confided that during the drug study, dozens of patients had been divided into four separate groups and treated with the identical drug and under identical conditions —everything, from the dosage to room décor to diet, was exactly the same. The only thing that varied was if, or how, an individual patient prayed.

The study found that the group of patients who never prayed and had no religious beliefs responded the least positively to the drug and were the slowest to heal, if they healed at all. The second group, which didn't pray but believed in a higher power, responded more positively to the drug than the nonbelievers and healed more quickly. An even better response was found in the patients who subscribed to a specific faith and prayed regularly.

But the far-and-away best response to the drug was found in the fourth group of patients, which happened to be those who prayed the rosary every day. Not only did the patients praying the rosary recover much faster than the others, but their group also had the highest percentage of patients who were completely cured!

My friend told me that the men and women of science overseeing this study were so perplexed by the results they contemplated handing out rosaries to every patient. But in the end their final report simply encouraged people to have faith in *something* when they become ill, because it seems that faith has the power to heal!

Of course, as you have witnessed again and again throughout this book, faith in God is the most powerful force we can ever hope to harness, and there is no better tool to direct that power into our lives than a sincerely prayed rosary. And yet the greatest gifts the rosary brings to us are the ones we never see . . . except in the smiles on the faces of those around us. The real miracles of the rosary are the miracles that the prayers and meditations perform within our souls. When we let God into our heart by praying the rosary, we have already experienced the greatest of all possible miracles, and everything else will take care of itself.

SHARING ALL THAT THE ROSARY has meant to me with you, dear friends, has been a great joy for me, and a blessing I will always cherish. I hope my story will inspire you to pick up some beads with the belief that, no matter how difficult your life may seem at times, the rosary will bring you peace and happiness.

With faith in our hearts and a rosary in our hands, we can find solutions to the little problems that crop up in our lives each day—and we will be able to triumph over even the greatest struggles and challenges we encounter, no matter how painful, difficult, or hopeless those struggles may seem.

As long as we pray the rosary with faith, everything we could ever want is within our reach, and happiness will never be more than a prayer away.

—·—

# ACKNOWLEDGMENTS

Thank you . . . to my dear God, the Father Almighty, for breathing life into me, for giving me my most loving Mother Mary to guide me and teach me to love you through the prayers of the rosary. Thank you, Dearest Mother, for your maternal love, and thank you for always rooting for all mankind. Thank you for the gift of this book, for making all things possible, and for saving my life—I love you.

— IMMACULÉE

A thousand thanks to my dear Immaculée, for your faith, friendship, and patience; thank you to Reid, Stacey, Shannon, Christy, Nick, and the rest of the Hay House team; a very special thanks to my good pal G. S. Bailey; thanks to Mary Schwarz, Father Walter, and my other friends at St. Vincent Ferrer; and a big thanks to Carmel Dyer and her sweet mum, Marie Veronica Dyer, for her helpful suggestions. And thanks, as always, to my beautiful wife, Natasha, my constant supporter and most beloved companion.

— STEVE

# ABOUT THE
# AUTHORS

**Immaculée Ilibagiza** was born in Rwanda and studied electronic and mechanical engineering at the National University. She lost most of her family during the 1994 genocide. Four years later, she immigrated to the United States and began working at the United Nations in New York City. She is now a full-time public speaker and writer. In 2007 she established the Left to Tell Charitable Fund, which helps support Rwandan orphans.

Immaculée holds honorary doctoral degrees from the University of Notre Dame and St. John's University, and was awarded the Mahatma Gandhi International Award for Reconciliation and Peace in 2007. She is the author, with Steve Erwin, of *Left to Tell, Led by Faith, Our Lady of Kibeho,* and *The Boy Who Met Jesus.*

To find out more about Immaculée and what she is doing to help spread God's messages of love, faith, and forgiveness, please visit: www.immaculee.com.

✢ ✢

**Steve Erwin** is a Toronto-born writer and award-winning journalist working in the print and broadcast media. Since moving to the United States in 2000, he worked several years as the New York correspondent for the Canadian Broadcasting Corporation and as a news/feature writer for *People* magazine. He co-authored the *New*

*York Times* best-selling memoirs *Left to Tell* and *Led by Faith* with Immaculée Ilibagiza, along with *Our Lady of Kibeho* and *The Boy Who Met Jesus*; as well as *The Gift of Fire* with Dan Caro. He lives in Manhattan with his wife, journalist and author Natasha Stoynoff.

—.—

# NOTES

# NOTES

# NOTES

# NOTES

## Hay House Titles of Related Interest

*YOU CAN HEAL YOUR LIFE, the movie,*
starring Louise L. Hay & Friends
(available as a 1-DVD program and an expanded 2-DVD set)
Watch the trailer at: www.LouiseHayMovie.com

*THE SHIFT, the movie,*
starring Dr. Wayne W. Dyer
(available as a 1-DVD program and an expanded 2-DVD set)
Watch the trailer at: www.DyerMovie.com

✣ ✣

*FROM PLAGUES TO MIRACLES: The Transformational Journey of
Exodus, from the Slavery of Ego to the Promised Land of Spirit,*
by Robert Rosenthal, M.D.

*I WANT TO SEE JESUS IN A NEW LIGHT: Healing Reflections
for People of All Faiths,* by Ron Roth, Ph.D.

*NO STORM LASTS FOREVER: Transforming Suffering Into Insight,*
by Dr. Terry A. Gordon

*PRACTICAL PRAYER: Using the Rosary to Enhance Your Life,*
by John Edward (book-with-CD)

*WISHES FULFILLED: Mastering the Art of Manifesting,*
by Dr. Wayne W. Dyer

All of the above are available at your local bookstore,
or may be ordered by contacting Hay House (see next page).

✣ ✣

We hope you enjoyed this Hay House book. If you'd like to receive our online catalog featuring additional information on Hay House books and products, or if you'd like to find out more about the Hay Foundation, please contact:

Hay House, Inc., P.O. Box 5100, Carlsbad, CA 92018-5100
(760) 431-7695 or (800) 654-5126
(760) 431-6948 (fax) or (800) 650-5115 (fax)
www.hayhouse.com® • www.hayfoundation.org

✦ ✦

*Published and distributed in Australia by:* Hay House Australia Pty. Ltd.,
18/36 Ralph St., Alexandria NSW 2015 • *Phone:* 612-9669-4299
*Fax:* 612-9669-4144 • www.hayhouse.com.au

*Published and distributed in the United Kingdom by:* Hay House UK, Ltd.,
Astley House, 33 Notting Hill Gate, London W11 3JQ • *Phone:*
44-20-3675-2450 • *Fax:* 44-20-3675-2451 • www.hayhouse.co.uk

*Published and distributed in the Republic of South Africa by:*
Hay House SA (Pty), Ltd., P.O. Box 990, Witkoppen 2068
*Phone/Fax:* 27-11-467-8904 • www.hayhouse.co.za

*Published in India by:* Hay House Publishers India, Muskaan Complex,
Plot No. 3, B-2, Vasant Kunj, New Delhi 110 070 • *Phone:* 91-11-4176-
1620 • *Fax:* 91-11-4176-1630 • www.hayhouse.co.in

*Distributed in Canada by:* Raincoast, 9050 Shaughnessy St., Vancouver,
B.C. V6P 6E5 • *Phone:* (604) 323-7100 • *Fax:* (604) 323-2600
www.raincoast.com

✦ ✦

**Take Your Soul on a Vacation**

Visit www.HealYourLife.com® to regroup, recharge, and reconnect
with your own magnificence. Featuring blogs, mind-body-spirit news,
and life-changing wisdom from Louise Hay and friends.

Visit www.HealYourLife.com today!

# Free e-newsletters
## from Hay House, the Ultimate
## Resource for Inspiration

Be the first to know about Hay House's dollar deals, free downloads, special offers, affirmation cards, giveaways, contests, and more!

 Get exclusive excerpts from our latest releases and videos from *Hay House Present Moments*.

 Enjoy uplifting personal stories, how-to articles, and healing advice, along with videos and empowering quotes, within *Heal Your Life*.

 Have an inspirational story to tell and a passion for writing? Sharpen your writing skills with insider tips from *Your Writing Life*.

## Sign Up Now!

*Get inspired, educate yourself, get a complimentary gift, and share the wisdom!*

## http://www.hayhouse.com/newsletters.php

**Visit www.hayhouse.com to sign up today!**

HealYourLife.com